Contender

Insider tips to crush your next job interview and negotiate a top salary

Authored by: Austin Fadely

Dedication

To my grandfather, Austin Francis Canfield, Jr., from whom I inherited the insatiable need to express myself regardless of the opinions of others, and who taught me the meaning of the word "logorrhea."

Table of Contents

Foreword 1

One: Be Professional 3

Two: Know Your Target 13

Three: Build an Online Presence and Stack the Odds 21

Four: Master the Interview 37

Five: Negotiate Your Salary and Benefits 51

Six: Kick Ass in Your First 90 Days 65

Conclusion 73

Interviews 75

About the Author 129

Foreword

This book is incredibly close to me because of the number of times I've had to look for a job. I did everything from online searches to going door to door. I've had to write and rewrite resumes, interview with a range of people, and wait for the callbacks.

Throughout my own career, I've had the opportunity to sit on both sides of the table. Everyone you interview with has been interviewed themselves. I've interviewed when I desperately needed a job to support my family. It's hard not to spill your life story when you feel like you have so much riding on the outcome. I also have been interviewed when I didn't need a job. It's a vastly different feeling when you can be a little choosey.

Even after all that experience applying for and taking jobs, I was blown away when I started interviewing people for this book. The advice I got was as diverse as it was surprising; however, some tips were consistent despite differences in industry. After all, all interviews are meant to determine if you can do the job and work with a team.

You might think of job hunting like a sparring match. You are up against stiff competition, and you need to be on your best game. Your resume lands you a chance at the title, and you have to show your best moves and throw your hardest punches to make it happen. You want to wow the interviewer and really knock them off their feet, but if you want the job title—if you want to be a true contender, don't think of it as a contest.

Job hunting is a lot more like dating. When a fight is over, it's over, but with a job, the hiring process is just the start of a relationship. The interview is a first date rather than a boxing match. You know a little about the company, and the company knows a little about you. You want to find out more about each other before you're willing to commit.

Some people are looking for a long-term relationship while others are interested in a fling to get them by until a better relationship comes along. Some people may never be interested in a long-term relationship. The same things that make a good relationship work are the same ones that make a good professional experience. There has to be respect, room to grow together, and hope for the future.

In much the same way, if you come to the table desperate and starved for a job, the less attractive you make yourself. You have to know your worth and not be upset if there is no second date. Some matches just aren't meant to be.

My purpose in this book isn't to give relationship advice: I wrote this to help a wide cross section of people who want to take the next step in their career but are a little nervous or unsure how to do it. Whether you're a recent grad or a seasoned professional looking for a change, I hope you find something of value here and transform yourself from hopeful job seeker to a true contender.

-Austin Fadely, April 2016

One: Be Professional

You only get one chance to make a first impression.

Artwork by Aron Daniels

The key to success in any career is professionalism. It's a lot like being courteous in a relationship; it should be common sense, but unfortunately it's not. I'm floored when I meet people with no sense of professionalism. Admittedly, I may be judging too harshly because it's not like there's a class (though there damn well should be). Not everyone has access to this sort of information, and a lot of what we take for granted as an unwritten rule isn't universally communicated.

Professionalism is an important topic to discuss, especially now that new trends are transforming the workplace. You see more informality in the way people want to work today. Working from home is rising in popularity now that technology can enable so many people to work remotely. You also see more flexibility in work schedules.

I think these are great changes. People should be able to work in an environment that makes them more productive, but there are times when you can be too familiar. It's important that we re-draw the lines to make them clear again.

Before you start looking for your next job, take some time to consider your own behavior in the workplace. Is it considered professional? Are there things you can improve?

Professionalism really boils down to two concepts: present yourself well, and follow through on your commitments. It may sound simple enough, but these principles should show in all of your work. That takes practice.

Present Yourself Well, Both Offline and Online

When an employer is prospecting you for a job, they're trying to decide if you'll follow their corporate philosophy. Each step in the hiring process is designed to find out more about you. It's critical that you are aware of how you appear to others.

Not every job requires that you wear traditional business attire. Some work places allow business casual (khakis and button downs). Others are more casual still. You dress to fit the culture where you work. But no matter what, you have to be hygienic and well groomed. Even if you wear jeans and a t-shirt to work, you don't want to show up scraggly and unkempt. You might be thinking this is obvious, but I've seen people that don't quite get it.

Appearance is more than just physical though. You have to behave professionally too. Every role requires that you have some degree of "soft skills" or people skills. You always have to work with other people, so you need to be able to communicate, work well under pressure, and keep calm. You have to help other people, and you have to have other people want to help you. This is what you're trying to convey through the course of the hiring process: you work well with others. That skill shows in your mannerisms, your approachability, and your willingness to have a conversation. You don't have to be the warmest, most extroverted person on the planet to knock an interview out of the park, but you do need to have a substantive conversation.

Through your conversation, you need to get across key selling points about yourself. I don't mean you start spouting off all the reasons you're awesome. I mean that you can demonstrate your competence simply by how you answer questions and what questions you ask. Interviewers don't want to hear you recite your resume; they want to get to know more about you.

Speaking of getting to know you, how does your online reputation look?

Professionalism is more than just dressing well and being on time; it is synonymous with character. You define yourself by your actions, but what you do isn't always in person or at the office. Today there is so much information a person can gather about you before ever meeting you. If you're serious about job searching, you'll have a LinkedIn account. From LinkedIn, a recruiter can Google your name and see what comes up. That will give them access to your Facebook account and other sites.

A lot of people feel like their Facebook and Twitter profiles are personal and shouldn't affect their professional lives. Although I tend to agree, there aren't any laws against it yet. On the flip side, companies tend to be (or try to be) hyper-aware of their branding. If employees are posting asinine things online, then it reflects poorly on the company. So remember, anything you are willing to put online is what you're willing to let a potential employer know about you.

Next time you're at a computer, Google yourself. See what comes up. Hopefully, you don't get some random photos a friend posted of you at a party. Some recruiters will find the pictures of you having a little too much fun and think you're irresponsible. Others might not care at all; however, if you're going for a client-facing position, then how you present yourself online can be a major concern, and some company may choose to pass you over based on some compromising pictures.

If your search turns up some questionable results, what can you do about it? Actually, there are a few things:

1. Make sure any information you control is made private or deleted. This includes Facebook accounts, Twitter, etc. This step should take care of the majority of embarrassing things. In those cases where you can't remove the content yourself, try reaching out to whoever owns the site or information about you and ask them to take it down. They might be YouTube videos, pictures, etc. Be respectful and explain why you need that information removed.

2. You also can try to knock the bad listings down in Google by filling up the top spots with information you want seen. Make new social media accounts on popular sites. Those are more likely to get top spot. Remember though that it takes time for Google's search engines to crawl sites, so making a new account right before an interview won't work. Do it now before you need to.

3. As a last resort, be prepared to explain anything that might make you look bad. Hopefully it's something you can explain away, like a picture that was taken a few years ago at a party.

Of course, your name may be common enough that this isn't a problem for you at all. For those of us with less common names, be aware of what your search results turn up. Even if you don't think you've done anything wrong, at least you'll know what's out there.

Email Etiquette

Communication is key in any profession. I assume you're intimately familiar with email and how it works, but poorly written emails cause more confusion and more work for everyone. Writing should be clear. This applies to all forms of writing…except poetry. A poorly written email makes the writer appear poorly educated or careless, neither of which are looked upon as great qualities. All the same rules of grammar apply to email as they do to writing letters, so use punctuation correctly.

First, have a professional-looking email address. This in and of itself says something about you. If you're a recent grad, I would recommend against using your student email. Gmail and Outlook both offer free email addresses, so it's incredibly easy to get one. Use something straightforward, like your full name and middle initial if need be.

You should also create an appropriate email signature. Make it easy for employers to get in contact with you if they choose to call. You can also add icons to your signature for LinkedIn or something like that, but don't overdo it with icons. Not everyone has images turned on in their email.

Also note that when sending an email from a smart phone, it will automatically attach a signature that says something like "Sent from my iPhone." I usually delete that line from my signature in favor of my name and my LinkedIn profile URL. When I'm emailing potential employers, I want to give the impression that I'm carefully considering my message rather than quickly shooting off an email from my phone. Not that emailing from your phone is frowned upon—it's just my personal preference. Either way you decide to have your signature, make sure you check your spelling and autocorrect before you send an email from your phone.

As for the rest of my email advice, some of it will apply to you as a job seeker, and the rest is for when you do land that job.

Don't use a whimsical font. Use something standard and professional like Calibri, Arial, Helvetica, etc. Same goes for font color and size. Regular messages should be in black font. Red is ok when editing or making inline comments for ease of reading. Usually the standard settings on your email work fine.

Don't send too many attachments. If you have say, more than 5 files, package them in a zip folder to make it easier for the recipient to organize. Some email programs, like Outlook, only show a few attachments at a time, and you have to scroll to see the rest—it's easy for some files to get missed. If you have to send several files separately, mention in the email how many there are.

Proofread before you send. Turn on spell check; make sure you spelled the person's name correctly (especially a potential employer). If you aren't sure of the spelling, use Google to search for the person. Type in what you think the name is and the company, or better yet, their email address. The first few results will usually give you what you need.

Don't use overly familiar language (including emojis :P LOLZ). When you're sending the first email to someone you don't know well, think business letter. This means addressing the person as Mr. or Ms., using a colon after the introduction, and ending with "Sincerely" or "Best Regards." If you are emailing a boss or potential client, let them set the tone of familiarity with first names, and always make sure your spelling is correct. No matter how familiar you may be with a boss or client, they will still evaluate you. You can be friendly, but always be professional.

Don't clutter work emails with nonsense or personal anecdotes. Depending on the company's culture, a sly joke or two for morale can be appropriate, but these should be few and far between in emails. Joking in person is fine, but you don't want to spam people's inbox with tons of non-work related stuff. Especially for emails with many recipients, an inside joke between two of you is not appropriate. Remember that other employees and your boss could see these emails. Then it looks like you're goofing off rather than working.

Don't use all caps. ALL CAPS ARE ANNOYING. The only appropriate time for caps is for acronyms like NATO, NAFTA, or USA. If something is really that urgent, say so in the subject line. "URGENT: subject line here."

Don't fire off several emails in a row. Nothing is more frustrating than trying to get some work done and suddenly some careless associate blows up your inbox. Be thoughtful about your emails, and take a minute to put everything you want to say in one or two emails.

Use descriptive subject lines. Email is a great resource to refer back to a conversation, especially when that conversation includes directions from your boss. Searching for those emails in a sea of hundreds (or thousands) is much more difficult when you don't use appropriate subject lines.

If you get an email about one subject and you have a question for the sender about a different subject, create a new conversation thread. You don't want to clutter a single thread with discussions not relevant to the initial email.

Social Networking

The internet has been around for years, but it has never before been as personal as it has over the past several. It seems nobody is complete without the internet, and it has thrust itself upon us with such success that any hope for higher education requires a plethora of typing skills, knowledge of computers, and internet access. The world is changing.

At first, it seems so cool. You can post pictures and write about yourself for others to see. You can write about your likes and dislikes; you can join interest groups, support causes, and invite people to events without leaving the comfort of your computer chair. But, unlike in real life, where you can alter your behavior to fit the circumstance, everyone sees what you do on the internet. It has become a total-networking experience.

There are several advantages to these sites: you can keep in touch with friends and post photos easily. The down side? It seems everyone is becoming so obsessed with these sites that it's now necessary to have two identities: real and cyber.

Your real identity is personal, and only people geographically close enough get to meet you. Your profile is a creation, a thing not exactly like you, but rather how you view yourself, and anyone can see it. Here is the problem: How many people have created profiles with little regard to what they put on them? Imagine that a smart, ambitious young prospective employee loses her shot because she didn't think about some picture her friend took at a party and tagged.

Make no mistake: people have lost jobs over what they have put on Facebook.

Recruiters and hiring managers are on social networks, and they will all be able to read your posts and see your pictures. Even if you engage your privacy settings (which you should be doing anyway) anyone can see your profile picture. The best practice is to be wary of how you present yourself online. I urge you to consider your profiles. What do you want the world to see?

Make sure you set your privacy settings on Facebook. Set up your profile so that people who don't know you can't see your posts or your friend's posts on your wall. That way, you control who can see what on your profile. Not sure how to do that? Google it.

There's a lot to consider as a job seeker. Remember that, just like dating, the core of the process is progressively revealing more about each other. As the company learns more about you, you learn more about the company. You get to choose how you present yourself. Hopefully, all goes well, and you'll get that second date.

Two: Know Your Target

Go where you are celebrated—not tolerated.

— Author Unknown

Job hunting these days is almost completely virtual (a bit like online dating). Nobody is really going out and "pounding the bricks" any more. There are still some industries where you can dress up, show up in person, fill out an application, and get hired. A lot of restaurants still let you do that, but if you're looking for a job to start or progress your career, you'll need to do some work online instead.

Getting the right job is more about fit than anything else. As you get older and your life circumstances change, so do your priorities and so does your sense of fit. To give you a personal example, as a single man, I was perfectly fine working as a 1099 contractor. The work was flexible, and I had a good income. I managed my own taxes, which was fine with me, and I had the most basic health insurance because I didn't need much. I didn't have any assets and didn't have life insurance. I had no issues working overtime or late into the night because I didn't have anyone to be responsible for other than myself.

Fast forward a few short years, and I have a wife and kids that depend on me (I was the sole breadwinner for our first few years as a family). Now that bare minimum health insurance just won't cut it, and neither will an unsteady stream of income. I value a good work-life balance more because I want to be home with my wife and kids. I also bought some life insurance and started putting money into a 401K—all that grown up crap.

Depending on what you value, your company targets will be different, and your ideal company may change over time. You may love a fast-paced tech start up with a work-hard play-hard attitude now, but a few years down the road, you might start to look for a seasoned Fortune 500 company with a more mature benefits package.

Picking a Company

Working for an employer is a relationship. There are tacit expectations on both sides, and if it's not meant to be, then hanging on to that relationship can be bad for everyone. That's why it's critical that you know yourself and know what you want.

Some people start with a list of companies they'd like to work for. That's a good start, but I would recommend doing more digging. The danger of starting with a specific company in mind is that you may underestimate something that's important to you that the company doesn't offer because you want to fit.

The other issue with this approach is that you can only list companies you know of, which rules out all the companies you don't. Pretty much every company I've worked for is one I'd never heard of before with few exceptions. My most fulfilling jobs have been at companies I only learned about during my job search.

A better approach is to start with a list of things you value. Build an archetype of what you prefer and weigh those categories. For example, do you prefer a corporate atmosphere or t-shirt and jeans? How important is that to you? Do you want a company with massive resources or one where you know everyone by name? Here some categories I'd start with:

Category	Weight (totals to 100)
Flexible work hours	8
Salary	25
Health & Family benefits	15
Commute Time	2
Ability to telecommute	2
Laid back culture	10
Upward mobility & clear pathway	10
Variety and fulfilling work	20
Time Off	8

You'll notice the weights add up to 100. This forces you to prioritize your categories. It's rare that you'll find a company that fits you perfectly that is also hiring and looking to fill a position you qualify for. Once you've made this chart, hang on to it. It will come in handy when you get to salary negotiations.

One thing I will emphasize here is honesty. You'll notice that I ranked salary as my number 1 priority. That doesn't make me greedy or money driven. A company that pays a lot of money but doesn't offer fulfilling work still gets a low score, but we all have bills, and we're lying if we say money isn't important. The whole reason we go to work for someone else is to earn money. We are trading our time and livelihood, so we can reasonably expect to be compensated for that.

This chart will change as your priorities change. For example, if you're currently not working, salary would rank very high. Then you run the risk of taking a job that pays you well but that leaves you unfulfilled. Chances are you'll be looking for another job in a relatively short amount of time. When you start looking for that next position, you need to readjust your chart. You get no benefits from lying about what motivates you, and your potential employer gets nothing out of hiring someone that wants to leave so soon.

Now that you have an idea of what type of company you'd like to work for, you can score them. At first, you can only judge them based on what you research. You never know everything about a company or a position until you actually have worked in it for several months. Still, you can do a lot of homework quite easily on any company you're considering. The first place I'd look is the website. Yes this is a corporate-controlled message, but you should know the values they intend to project. This will give you some good questions to ask when you start talking to employees.

Next, try to get some candid reviews. Glassdoor.com has loads of reviews you can reference. Indeed.com does as well. You can also seek out employees, and see if they'll be willing to give you some insight into the company culture and values. Start by searching LinkedIn to see if you have any 1st or 2nd degree contacts that work there. Ask them how well they think the company achieves its mission statement (which you should have read on the website).

Bear in mind that there are negative reviews for every company. Try to figure out if the bad review was because of a personal experience (bad relationship with a single colleague or boss) or a symptom of the culture.

Picking a Role

More than just knowing what company you want to work for, you need to know what role you're looking for. You may not know the exact title, but you should be able to describe what you'd like to do. This is actually pretty tough if you're recently out of college and not familiar with the work force yet. So when you envision your ideal job, remember to be flexible in terms of what you take at entry level. You can always work towards your goals.

Once you have some experience, you'll be better able to describe your ideal role because you'll know what to compare it to. When you get to that point, you can hold out for what you're looking for because by then, you should know enough to get hired for it.

When you're looking to get hired, part of what you need to do is evaluate the company. The other part you need to do is figure out what the role is. Some companies may be hiring for a number of roles, so it will be on you to describe to them what you'd like to do. In other cases, the company may be looking for a specific type of candidate for one role they have. You need to know at a high-level what you want to do and what kind of company you'd like to work for.

When you do figure out the role you'd like, make sure any information about you on your resume and LinkedIn profile emphasize that point. Don't clutter your resume and confuse people with things that you did but aren't necessarily what you want to do. You may be great at accounting, but don't list it as a skill if you hate doing it.

You get what you put out there, so put out what you want to do, and that's what you'll eventually get.

Three: Build an Online Presence and Stack the Odds

"Well Roy, your application was impressive,
but I saw your last profile status,
and I just can't hire you after that."

Artwork by Aron Daniels

If you're looking for a job now, you have to be online, and you have to be on LinkedIn. Every recruiter I've spoken to has mentioned LinkedIn as the primary resource behind employee referrals. I used LinkedIn to get a job in 2013 and again in 2014.

The great thing about having a good LinkedIn profile is that it works two ways. Sometimes recruiters will reach out to you, and you can use LinkedIn to narrow down your job search. I'm a big fan of the platform, and I actually provide a link to my profile in my digital resume.

LinkedIn

LinkedIn is continually improving. They recently allowed profiles to have videos as part of their profile summaries. I always do my best to keep my LI up to date for several reasons: first and foremost, it makes you more visible. Got a new skill? Add it. Make a new contact? Connect with them. Finished another project? Describe it.

You can put so many things that you just can't fit on a one or two-page resume. I list out projects, people I've worked with, classes I took in school, volunteer activities... everything. The one thing companies look for is fit, and the best way for them to ascertain that before hiring you is to see what kind of work you've done. Titles are ambiguous because they rarely mean the same things across different companies. The best information you can provide are examples of projects and accurate descriptions of what the project was and what you did on them.

That isn't to say to put everything on there you can think of. Be selective about what you write. The difference between an amateur and a professional is that an amateur shows you all of her work, but a professional shows you her best work. Remember that you get what you put out there, so if you're putting a ton of detail into a job you hated, you may get contacted about that type of work. Accentuate your strengths and where you'd like to go.

LinkedIn lets you list out what classes you've taken in addition to the degree you've earned. I use that to show what classes I took for my MBA and a few that I thought may be relevant from my undergraduate degree. There's no penalty for putting this information on there, and you don't know what may be the tipping point between getting a call or not.

One of the best tools I've come across is LinkedIn's jobs tool. You can search and narrow down jobs based on keywords, title, company, geographic location, etc. Advanced search features let you pick job functions, salary, and industry. You can get really granular in your choices, and you can save opportunities to review later.

Some of the jobs listed also have a one-click apply with LinkedIn button. I love those, and for a while, I would exclusively apply to those jobs because I could do 15-20 of them in an hour. That's a much better rate than having to fill out an individual form on every website you visit. Applying for jobs is a numbers game, so the more you apply, the more calls you get. You're building a sales funnel for yourself, so any way to put more applications out there with less work is a plus.

Job Boards

Job boards provide good ways to search for your next career as well. Sites like monster.com, glassdoor.com, and indeed.com are quite popular. There are also industry specific job boards you should look into. For example, if you're in IT, you should be looking at dice.com.

The trick with job boards is there isn't much to differentiate yourself aside from your resume. LinkedIn is more of a social network, so you can post relevant information like past projects, people you've worked with, and recommendations as well as your resume. You can even make blog posts. There's more for you to showcase. On a job board, you pretty much get to name your location, salary range, and post a resume.

That's not to say that it's not worth going to sites like that. Recruiters are still there and job postings are still there. I personally have never had success with job boards, but I also chose to spend more time making my LI profile more robust. Like anything, you get out what you put in.

Resumes

The most important thing you can do for yourself is make damn sure you have a solid resume. It's your pickup line. You want to draw attention in a positive way so that you get the call back.

With so many ways you can apply for jobs today, resumes take on many different forms, but the common theme no matter your presentation is content. Make sure what you put down is relevant to what you want to do. Each line should have a specific purpose. If it isn't adding to your chances of getting an interview, it can stand to be cut.

Writing a good resume is somewhat of an art form. In one or two pages, you must highlight your skills, knowledge, abilities, education, and experience. There is no secret formula to writing a resume because it depends on the job, your level of experience, and what you feel the need to emphasize. That being said, there are a few helpful guidelines you should follow.

Put the most impressive and relevant information about you at the top. If you work in an industry where you're required to have a lot of certifications, you may put that at the top. You may instead decide to put skills if that suits your goals. If you're fresh out of college, you might consider putting your education towards the top. Think of it this way, if a recruiter only reads the top half of your resume, what do you want them to remember about you? There's a surprising amount of flexibility in presentation.

Make sure you list skills that are specific to your industry. Don't shy away from jargon. For example, my resume has UI/UX on it. I wouldn't expect someone outside of web development technology to understand that, but I can reasonably expect people in my industry to get it. It's also a lot more of a space saver than "User Interface/User Experience."

Whatever you put on your resume, be sure you can back it up. Lying about your skills wastes everyone's time, including your own. If you say you have project management experience, be prepared to discuss projects you've managed (both successful and unsuccessful ones). If you list that you do web design, have some links to live websites you worked on. As an aside, any time you link to work in your resume, make sure you check them before you send them out. Nothing says lazy quite like a few links to broken sites.

Don't list every little accomplishment. You simply do not have enough room to include absolutely everything. Instead, think of what would be most relevant.

When possible, quantify your experience. For instance:

> "supervised a marketing team of three" is better than "supervised a marketing team."

> "raised sales by 3% and brought in an additional $100,000" is better than "raised sales while at the company."

Lazlo Bock, Senior VP at Google, has a great LinkedIn article where he describes his formula of "Accomplished [X] as measured by [Y] by doing [Z]."

Companies are big on measurable performance and return, so if you can quantify your accomplishments by stating what goals you met and how you met them, you have a more powerful statement.

One myth I've come across is that many people think you have just one resume. That's simply not true. You may be applying to many different types of jobs. Your skill set in one area may not be relevant in another, so you'll want a resume that highlights your applicable skills for each type of job. For example, if I were to apply to be a marketing director, I would highlight my experience in marketing. If I wanted to stick with project management, those are the skills and experiences I would emphasize.

Back in 2010 and briefly for 2012, I held a few part time jobs. I had some resumes that listed some of the part time jobs, and I had others that didn't. I was going after some slightly different roles within the same industry, so I needed resumes with different content. I spent some time as a part-time salesperson for computers. Whenever I applied to a job that was more sales oriented, I included my sales position. When I applied to a job that was more operations oriented, I left the computer sales job off because I needed that space to accentuate other skills.

If you're just starting to search for a job, it can be overwhelming to write up so many different resumes off the bat. I'd recommend starting with a base resume, one that captures the core of your talents. As you start seeing other jobs you're interested in, modify your base resume and save it for the role-type you're looking for. The first few times it will feel tedious. You'll be constantly writing and tweaking several different versions, but given time, you'll have a resume for most every job you want.

In terms of length, I've heard different rules, but one I like to follow as a guide is 10 years per page. If you have been working 10 years, you can probably fit most everything on to a single page. After that amount of experience, you can move on to two pages, but I'd never go past two. If you need more than two pages to sell yourself, you're not selling yourself well. Now the 10 years per page rule isn't carved in stone. If you have a varied but applicable skill set and experiences, don't be afraid to bleed onto page two. Now that the average length of time someone sticks with a company is two years, you may very well have quite a bit of things to cover with only six years' experience.

If you do go on to a second page, don't feel like you need to fill it up. You should only cover what's relevant. (Yes, I'm repeating myself but it's that important!) Now let's say you do take a second page, and it's only two or three lines. In that case, I challenge you to cut your first page down a little bit. Your second page should still be substantive.

For the love of all that is holy, do not decrease your margins, line height, and font size just to adhere to a page limit. All that does is create visual tension. Your resume has to be scan-able. Recruiters and hiring managers have a lot of papers to work through, and you don't want to make them feel like they're reading James Joyce to try to figure out if you're a fit. Keep comfortable spacing.

Grammar is critical. Some recruiters have flat out told me that they won't bother with people who can't proof their own resumes. That not only means your spelling is correct; it also means your bullet points have parallel structure, and you're consistent with verb tense. You'll be particularly embarrassed if you say you have "significant attention to detail," and you have a big, fat typo. Speaking of attention to detail, don't fill your resume with useless crap like "significant attention to detail." Find things of substance to say about yourself. Your job descriptions should demonstrate whether or not you're attentive.

If you speak English as a second language, some recruiters may be more forgiving, but you can still have someone proofread your resume for you.

Once you've got your content rock solid, it's time to put some finishing touches to the design to bring it all together. Everyone has different preferences. I tend to use dark red lines to highlight my resume. Used sparingly, it makes the resume pop a little without being too much. For my line of work, it's acceptable. I also used a color that I knew would print to gray and still look good from a black and white printer. Remember that your resume might be viewed either digitally or printed out. If you have a hyperlink in your resume, write out the entire link rather than just a word or phrase.

You may be tempted to use non-traditional fonts to set yourself apart. Don't. Less is more. Especially for the body content, stick to standard fonts like Times, Calibri, or Helvetica. You can be a little more creative with your headings though. I like to use serif fonts for my headings and sans-serif fonts for the body text. Still, unless you know the company culture is off-beat, stay away from outlandish fonts.

I also like to use tables with invisible borders. This lets me create columns in sections of the Word document. It will take some work, but it's a good payoff to have an exceptional looking resume. A good design makes you look more professional; however, no amount of design will overcome a bad skill fit or poor content.

Above all, the resume should be easy to scan and effectively highlight your relevant strengths. Recruiters are looking for positional fit. They want to make sure you have the experience to do the job they're hiring for. There is a saying in web content writing—give the people what they want when they want it. Make reading your resume easy and not a chore. You can see an example of my resume and an old cover letter (with identifying information removed) at the end of the chapter.

Cover Letter

Many companies require a cover letter along with your resume. If you are sending out resumes unsolicited, include a cover letter automatically. The letter introduces you, allows you to create a more personal touch, and complements your resume. Do not repeat yourself across the two documents. If you're going to replicate your resume in paragraph form, you may as well not send one.

Cover letters are supposed to be unique and personal for each job. Each one you send out should be slightly different, but if you write one letter focusing on your skills and how you can benefit a company, you can get away with having a single base letter and simply tweak the language for different companies. This will save you time when applying. If you're going after different types of jobs, ones that require different skill sets, then you can have a different base letter for each type.

There are different types of cover letters. A cover letter for a known job opening will clearly identify the job for which you are applying. A prospecting cover letter asks if there is an opening, and a networking cover letter requests more information or help in your job search. If you post your cover letter on a Website, your purpose will be prospecting, since you're asking for a job but may not know who is looking at your cover letter.

A good cover letter should be enthusiastic and confident. It will explain why you are interested in the company and job as applicable. You should highlight and explain your most relevant skills. Be sure to emphasize how those skills would benefit the company.

For all cover letters, follow the same format as a business letter. The first paragraph should clearly state what position you are applying for (or what position you'd like to have) and what drew you to the company. Use the opening paragraph as an opportunity to show exactly why you're excited to work for them. The next few paragraphs should underscore how your relevant abilities align with the company's corporate strategy (which you can try to figure out from their website and client list). How will your strengths help get the company ahead? Remember that you want to make yourself valuable enough to hire. Finally, leave some room to follow up and make your availability clear to the reader.

As with your resume, pay attention to the format. Is it on paper or is it electronic? If on paper, make sure you use the same stock paper for everything you send in, and use good quality paper. You want to appear professional.

The Follow-Up Letter

Follow-up letters are not crucial. These days, you can easily follow up with an email, but if you really want to give that extra flair, send a letter if you don't hear back from an application. That might be the edge you need to get called in for an interview. Remember that jobs don't just come to you; you have to be aggressive if you want to stand out from the throng of other applicants.

The purpose of the follow-up letter is to "move your resume to the top of the pile," so to speak. Finding a new hire can take weeks for a company. If you get your resume and cover letter in early, you may not hear back for some time. Generally, if you haven't heard within a week and a half, send a follow-up; however, if the company explicitly states that all candidates will be contacted by a certain date, it would be inappropriate to send a follow-up before that date. Otherwise, take the opportunity for the "touchpoint."

Use the same format as your cover letter (business letter format) and mention that you have sent in the resume. Remind them of who you are and why you would be a good employee. Follow-up letters are short and to the point.

As I said, you could send an email in lieu of a letter, but bear in mind that the person you are contacting may have several emails in her inbox. Your contact person may accidentally delete your email before ever reading it. A paper letter is much more likely to be noticed and appreciated than an email, which is gone in the click of a button. That isn't to say emails are not effective, but make sure you use a good subject line. For example something like "Follow up on position x application" clearly states what the email is about and is short enough that it can be viewed on most any email client.

Austin Fadely

xxx.xxx.xxxx
austinfadely@gmail.com

Objective: To join a group of innovators, apply my creative skills and analytical abilities, and manage high-performing teams in a fast-paced and challenging environment.

Education

M.B.A. – Wake Forest University Schools of Business	Grad: Aug. 2014	GPA: 3.8 *Beta Gamma Sigma*
B.A. Eng. Communications – UMBC	Grad: Dec. 2007	GPA: 3.6 *Cum Laude*

Relevant Skillset

- Project management
- Agile/SCRUM/Waterfall
- Resource management
- Risk management
- Continuous process improvement

- Business intelligence
- Cross-functional team management
- Client communication
- Organization and coordination

- Web marketing
- Web technologies
- CSS, HTML, JS, MySQL
- CRM/CMS/UX/UI
- CPQ/ERP/Back office

Certifications

- Salesforce Certified Administrator
- Salesforce Certified Developer

- Salesforce Service Cloud Certified
- PROS Price Optimizer Configuration

- PROS Scientific Analytics Configuration

Professional Experience

Acumen Solutions   McLean, VA   **Senior Consultant:** Nov 2014–present

- Engage clients in conversation regarding requirements, scope, and project planning. Act as primary point of contact for client project managers and product owners; relay project status and explain technical constraints to inform better decision making. Serve as first level of escalation for project team concerning potential impacts to project scope and timeline.
- Manage communication across multiple project teams, client offices, and third party vendors.
- Manage a team of developers, QA testers, and architects to drive projects successfully to completion. Team sizes range from 6-15, project budgets range from $0.5-1.1M.
- Participate in and facilitate high-level design and solution discussions to ensure proper business rules and logic are being met.
- Develop project plans, manage risk, run project meetings and agile ceremonies, and manage resources to ensure successful delivery of iterative code development.
- Assist with business development activities for public sector clients. Specific examples include helping design and test a responsive web form using open source technologies for a federal agency as part of an RFP process.
- Gather relevant case studies and put together tailored presentations demonstrating the company's relevant knowledge and capabilities. Clients include both public and private sector.

Beacon Technologies   Greensboro, NC   **Project Manager:** May 2013–Oct 2014

- Managed several projects from start to finish, acted as clients' primary contact, and managed multiple teams of up to 10 employees including designers, developers, and digital marketers.
- Maintained open lines of communication with existing clients to generate future business opportunities and manage service level agreements.
- Performed quality checks and browser/device testing for responsive websites. Conducted market research to set company policy regarding device testing.

Want to know more? Follow me on LinkedIn!
http://www.linkedin.com/in/austinfadely

- Managed project timelines, requirements gathering, technical assessments, estimates, budgets, and risk analyses.
- Understood components of various web-based programming languages such as SQL, Classic ASP, .NET, HTML5, CSS3, JavaScript, and communicated technical nuances to clients.

Self-Employed   Kernersville, NC   **Freelance Web Designer:** Feb 2013–May 2013
- Designed and coded websites that fulfilled functional requirements set by clients.
- Used Adobe Creative Suite including Photoshop, Illustrator, InDesign, and Fireworks.
- Coded websites in HTML5, CSS3, JavaScript, and PHP.

Rhino Graphica, LLC.   Kernersville, NC   **Project Manager:** 2010–2012
- Managed set up, configuration, and training for various CRM and CRM combination platforms for the company and specific clients; platforms included Salesforce, ActiveCollab, and Worketc.
- Interacted with, presented reports, and demonstrated software products to senior management at client companies. My contacts' titles included VPs of Marketing and C-level executives.
- Ran weekly internal meetings as well as set up and conducted status meetings with clients.
- Wrote all project documentation including Requirements Docs, Contracts, Change Orders, and managed all workflow items using a combination of CRM and Project Management Software.
- Managed four employees, external teams, and worked with a diverse international group.
- Developed compiled, and analyzed a wide variety of reports including consumer insights, email marketing performance, e-commerce, ROI, and Website/Web-platform traffic.

Want to know more? Follow me on LinkedIn!
http://www.linkedin.com/in/austinfadely

Austin Fadely

###.###.###
austinfadely@gmail.com

My Street Address
City Name, NC 12345

Beacon Technologies
164 Thatcher Road
Greensboro, NC 27409

April 23, 2013

Dear Hiring Manager:

I am thrilled about the Project Manager opportunity at Beacon Technologies. You have an impressive client list, and I'm excited to see the company taking on more responsive web design projects. Mobile browsing is a tremendous growth area.

As a small, yet well-established company, Beacon Technologies needs somebody familiar with both the technology and marketing sides of the industry. Having a great website with no marketing is like spending all day cooking a fantastic Thanksgiving dinner and forgetting to invite everyone. This is something Beacon clearly understands, and it needs employees that understand so that your clients are better served.

As a project manager for Rhino Graphica, I am familiar with the logistics of running a project from start to finish, including managing resources, budget, timelines, and risks. Because Rhino Graphica was such a small organization, I gained hands-on experience with email marketing tools, social network marketing, and search engine optimization.

I am an avid learner, and I continually push myself to learn new concepts and master new skills. As Beacon Technologies grows to take on new responsive web projects and expand its client base, it will need someone who can grow with the company, take on different responsibilities as needs arise, and adapt to the latest trends and developments in the industry.

Thank you for your thoughtful consideration.

Best Regards,

[Signature Redacted]

Austin Fadely

Four: Master the Interview

"Are you ready for the final phase
of your interview, Mr. Smith?"

Artwork by Aron Daniels

If you make it to the interview, that's a great sign. The company thinks you might be a fit, and they want to be sure. Good interviewers are trying to assess two things: does your experience match your resume, and are you a good fit culturally with the company?

The first part shouldn't worry you as long as you didn't lie on your resume. Be prepared to answer questions about past experiences relating to the work you might end up doing at that company. Be truthful about your limitations, and be prepared to explain how you can overcome them.

You need to do some prep work before you walk into the interview. Showing up unprepared is the worst thing you can do, next to being poorly dressed.

Be Early

There is a saying: if you're on time, you're late. Arriving ahead of schedule shows that you respect that your interviewer is taking time out of her work schedule to meet with you. You know that her time is valuable, so you want to make sure you don't throw off the rest of her day. In fact, the interviewer may cut the session short or refuse to see you at all if you're late.

Another reason to be early is to provide some cushion for unexpected delays. It may rain the day of your interview. There could be a traffic accident, or you might just get every red light on the road. You never know, so leave early.

Make sure you include time to park, walk to the building, and get to the correct office. Don't make the mistake of measuring time to get from one place to the other by drive time only. You really should be measuring the time it takes to get your butt in the interview chair.

If you've never been to the company's office before, you run a high risk of getting lost the day of the interview. There's nothing quite as nerve wracking as frantically trying to find an unfamiliar office the day of your interview. GPS navigators are not correct 100% of the time; not to mention, they are not very precise. If your interview happens to be near a busy road with an overpass, good luck. That's why you should go to the office a day or two before your interview. Familiarize yourself with the area so that when it comes time to head out, you know exactly where to go. In larger office buildings, you can also go inside and try to find the office. What floor is it on? Where are the elevators?

Program the company contact number into your phone. If it turns out it's hard to navigate the area, call and get directions. Try to get your interviewer's number as well and program that in.

If you are going to be late, call your interviewer right away. Apologize for not making it on time and have a good, truthful reason. Car trouble, for instance, is often unpredictable, so there's a measure of understanding. Even so, you can do your part to take extra precautions. If in doubt of your car's wellbeing, you may want to make sure your car can start two hours before you have to leave just in case you need to make other arrangements. Call when you know you are going to be late, not at interview time. Absolutely do not wait until after to call. It's unprofessional.

Presentation

You only get one shot to make a first impression. Yes, it's a cliché, but what you wear to an interview says a lot about you. Dressing appropriately can make or break a first impression. A person who looks put together clearly pays attention to detail, and that is exactly what you want to get across.

Fashion is about you and your style. It's how you want to portray yourself to the world. Whatever you decide, you should choose to wear clothes that complement your figure, height, and complexion. Some fashions make you look taller while others can make you look larger. It's important to know which looks work for you and which don't.

This is not intended to be a fashion advice book. The only reason I bring it up is because I've seen some people that are absolutely clueless on how to dress for an interview. There aren't any classes on dress etiquette, so I think it's important to cover some basic concepts.

Men's Wear

Nobody is born knowing fashion, so take some time and figure out what flatters your body type. There is a lot of information out on the internet. I encourage you to explore and learn. I'll focus on a few of the major points here, but this is certainly not exhaustive.

For interviews, I'm a big fan of suits. Many new companies might feel that traditional office wear is boring and outdated. Lots of startups focus on ideas rather than appearance. Mark Zuckerburg, CEO and founder of Facebook, often appears at conferences in jeans and a T-shirt or hooded sweatshirt. Knowing your prospective company's culture will help you figure out what to wear. Notable exceptions aside, nobody will think less of you for wearing a suit. In fact, you only stand to gain from dressing well. Dress for the job you want, not the job you have.

Another cool thing about suits is that if you take off the tie and undo the top button of your shirt, you're still dressed up but in a more casual style.

Suits come in several styles, colors, and patterns. Your first suit is a big investment. To start, I recommend charcoal gray. It's versatile and goes with a lot of different dress shirts. You'll get plenty of use out of a dark suit with a traditional cut. Fads go out of style, but classic looks are timeless; plus, you can wear the suit to other events.

Nothing fits quite like a tailored suit, but unless you have a good chunk of change to throw down, you'll have to shop off the rack. Make sure you go to a store with knowledgeable professionals, so they can take your measurements. Fit is the most important thing for a suit (or anything for that matter). Get one that matches your body type. Just because something looks good on a model or a mannequin doesn't mean it will work for you.

If you aren't into the suit look, or if you're not sure if the company you're applying for would consider it too dressy, you can always ask the person coordinating your interview. If the company seems pretty traditional, then it's safe to go with a suit. If you're applying for a trendy start up with a laid back culture, don't be shy about asking what to wear. Some companies might say jeans and your favorite Tee are fine.

Women's Wear

There's a lot more variety for women's wear, which makes it harder to write about. When going for a professional look, it's best to dress conservatively. You can go with a full suit, a long skirt with a blouse, or any number of combinations. The important thing is to dress elegantly and professionally, so no jeans or low cut tops.

Again, the key element is fit. If you've never had to dress for a professional interview before and aren't sure what types of clothes to wear, find a decent department store with knowledgeable sales staff.

The same rules apply though: dress for your height, body type, and complexion. Find a style that complements your favorite features about yourself. It will give you a confidence boost for the interview if you like the way you look.

Tattoos and Piercings

We are living in an ever more progressive world. More companies are open to a more casual look, and this includes tattoos and piercings. Other companies prefer to remain more conservative in terms of appearance. It is entirely up to you what kind of environment you'd like to work in, but make sure to dress appropriately for the type of work you're going to do.

If you're going into a client-facing role where you'll be representing the company, chances are you'll need to at least be able to cover your tattoos and piercings. If you're applying for a more back-office type role, then you might be fine. Use discretion, but be true to yourself. If you hate the idea of covering up your ink, then don't apply for jobs that will make you.

The Interview

Make sure you are prepared going into the interview. Turn off your cell phone and have extra copies of your resume. Many companies require you to apply online, and your interviewer may not have that information in front of her. You demonstrate your foresight when you can provide things quickly. Make sure to keep your papers in something sturdy, and do not hand your interviewer a creased up resume with a coffee stain on it. Also make sure you print extras well before you have to leave for your interview. You don't need the stress of having your printer break ten minutes before you have to be out the door.

Don't stress too much about the interview. Again, hiring managers are really just looking for a couple things: does your skill set match your resume and are you a good fit culturally? A little bit of nervousness from you is understandable, so don't beat yourself up over it and make it worse.

When a company is trying to assess your technical skills, you'll usually interview with somebody familiar with the work you are applying to do. They'll ask you situational questions. You can prepare for these by thinking about some common scenarios, such as a time you overcame some difficulty with a project, co-worker, or client. Remember that you are demonstrating your professionalism and ability to handle difficulty. Don't bad-mouth anyone in your interview. You can describe a situation as frustrating, but not a person.

You'll most likely get asked about a weakness. Be honest, but don't be detrimental. If you're applying for a client-facing position, don't say things like, "I have a short fuse when it comes to stupid clients." Take the opportunity to describe how you're working to improve that weakness. Everyone has things they don't do well, but showing that you are working to make yourself better means that you'll be an asset that's always increasing value to the company.

Cultural fit is pretty subjective. When you're being asked questions about culture, you should try to assess the company as well. You don't want to work at a place that's not a good fit for you. Hopefully, the research you did before agreeing to the interview will give you some insight into the company culture. The types of questions in these interviews can be situational and personality-driven. Hiring managers may want to explore how you react to pressure, how you deal with and work through conflict, and what your personal values are. Don't say what you think the interviewer wants to hear. Be confident in your values. If at the end of the interview, the hiring manager doesn't think your values are a good fit for the company, why would you want to work for them?

Try to establish a rapport with your interviewer. Smile, be courteous and energetic, and look the person in the eye. Give the interviewer a firm handshake and take note of your tone. Sit up straight and be positive. It's tough to remain optimistic when you've applied for several jobs already, but the interviewer doesn't know how many jobs you've applied to. Act like it's the first one. You can do a lot to set the tone of the interview just by your countenance.

People have a tendency to mimic the mood around them. If you're dull and lethargic, the interviewer will not only know it, she'll feel it. A good mood is contagious, so act excited and thrilled about being called in for an interview. Remember that the person across the desk conducts interviews for a good reason; they are a good judge of character. Make sure your good character shines through. Be genuine.

If you're new to interviewing or haven't done it in a while, remember that it's ok to be a bit nervous. Just take a deep breath and speak clearly. People don't like it when they have to strain to hear what you're saying. Speaking too quietly can make a person uncomfortable and annoyed. Worse yet, you appear less confident. Speak up and be heard. If an interviewer is constantly asking you to repeat yourself, be a little louder. If you look the person in the eye, you'll have more of a tendency to speak at an audible level.

Also consider that you may be talking too quickly. This is easy to do when you're nervous. I actually tend to speak so quickly that I begin to breathe heavy. Just take a moment and breathe. Don't sweat it. Just relax and focus on being calm.

Try not to say "um, like, you know," or any familiar slang. Speak like a professional. Say "hello" or "hi" and not "hey." If you're struggling to think of an answer to a question, take a moment in silence to think. Don't feel like you have to fill silence with noise. It's easy to slip into a casual speech, especially when you hear it a lot from your friends. For practice, try telling a story to yourself before the interview without using empty words.

Don't take too long to make your point. Listen to each question carefully, and answer them fully. Your first sentence should be to answer the question. After that, you can elaborate. Give yourself the opportunity to offer relevant information, but don't ramble on about anything that doesn't make your position stronger.

On the other hand, you don't want your answers to be too short. If you answer open-ended questions with one or two words, then you aren't thinking about the question. The interviewer isn't going to know all the right questions to ask, so volunteer information that makes you a stronger candidate.

Be prepared to answer tough questions. A common one you may come across will be why you left your last job. (It really helps if you weren't fired from it.) Again, no badmouthing—it will only make you look immature and unprofessional.

Some interviewers will ask questions to test your knowledge. If you don't know the answer, don't try to lie your way through it. A lot of learning is done on the job and in training. Not knowing the answer to a question is not an interview killer, but not answering questions truthfully is.

Try to be aware of your nonverbal cues. Ask people you can trust to be honest with you about any habits you have that come across as cold or unapproachable. To give you an example, my neutral face looks angry. I've had plenty of people, including my wife, ask me what I'm angry about when I'm just sitting there thinking.

When I meet with people, I consciously turn the outside of my mouth up a little. It's not quite a smile, but it softens my expression. I found this eases people's perception of me and makes me more approachable. You might have some habits you need to tweak, like crossing your arms or clicking your tongue.

If you find yourself doing some of these things in the interview, don't overreact. Calmly and casually adjust your behavior.

These are things you should be aware of and practice, but don't get so caught up in your body language that you get flustered. If you're a good fit and have the skill set, you'll be fine. Monitoring your body language is less of a core strategy than it is a fine-tuning technique.

Finally, do your best to relax. Remember, interviewers expect a little bit of nervousness, so don't beat yourself up if you trip up or speak too quickly. Just take a deep breath and power forward. Be sure to smile and thank the interviewer as you leave.

Flip the Script

Be prepared with a list of questions for your interviewer. Spend some time and think of unique and specific challenges the company faces and ask questions about it. Probe deep. You not only show that you'd take the job seriously, you're also showing your analytical capabilities. If you really want to impress your interviewer, ask awesome questions and make them feel like you're interviewing them.

For the types of questions to ask, steer away from salary and compensation. You'll have plenty of time to discuss that if and when you get an offer. You don't want to discuss salary too early, and if it does come up, politely say that it would be better to discuss that once both you and the company have gotten a better chance to learn more about each other.

Instead ask questions about the corporate mission (but don't ask what their corporate mission is; you'll appear foolish if it's on the website and you didn't bother to look).

Here is a list of questions you can start with, but feel free to come up with your own:

1. What are some new challenges the company faces this year that it hasn't before?
2. What would you say is the most critical thing I could do in my first week here?
3. What does success look like for this company next year?
4. Do you have a formal mentorship program? How does one get involved?
5. How did you get involved with the company and what makes you stay?

Although you can come up with several questions beforehand, you might want to come up with a few based on the content of the interview. If the interviewer said something that you want to dig into a bit more, take the opportunity to ask.

The type of questions you ask will also depend on your experience level.

If you're new to the work force or new to the industry, you should ask questions about the industry. Who does the company view as their top competitors?

If you've been in the industry a while and know the ropes, you may have more company-specific questions. For example, what does this company do successfully that other competitors don't?

Be ready with good questions and lots of them. Make sure what you're asking reflects well on your research. Don't ask basic stuff for the sake of taking up air. Get beyond because that's how you'll stand out.

For some extra ammunition, try to research your interviewer on LinkedIn before the interview. Don't be shy about bringing up something from your interviewer's past experience. Ask something like, "I saw on LinkedIn that you used to work at this other company. Did you find that there were a lot of transferrable skills that helped you succeed here or did you have to re-learn everything the company way?" Interviewers and hiring managers love it when you do research, so any bit of information you have, like the name of your interviewer, can give you an edge. I would recommend against stalking their Facebook however. LinkedIn is fine because it's a professional network for the purpose of connecting with other professionals. Facebook is personal.

The Thank You Card

Always write a thank you card. It's a dying art, and it will help to set you apart. It won't make up for a misalignment of skills or a bad cultural fit, but it might be enough to give you an edge otherwise.

The thank you letter can be a card or just simple correspondence thanking your interviewer for the opportunity to meet with her. You not only show above average professionalism, you show an ethic to follow things through.

This letter should be personal. You have already met and made contact, so you can be a little less formal. Hand writing a card or writing a thank you with a similar outline as your cover letter are both acceptable practices. When used in conjunction, your cover letter and resume, follow up letter, interview, and thank you card put your name in your employer's mind at least four times. It doesn't guarantee you the job, but it doesn't hurt to have your interviewer remember you.

I prefer physically writing the thank you card as opposed to sending an email, and the reason is effort and rarity. I have a stack of generic thank you cards that I keep on hand. It's quick to write something up and drop it in the mail, but it shows you put more thought and effort into your thanks than a simple email, which takes seconds to do and requires little thought. A thank you card isn't something interviewers see every day, so it stands out more.

In the end, if you have the right skill set, can demonstrate integrity, and display a team-mentality, you'll probably get hired. No amount of prep work and interview tricks will get you hired if you can't do the job. These tips are here to help you present the best version of yourself and improve your chances assuming that you are a good fit. They can also help give you the edge over other, less polished candidates.

Five: Negotiate Your Salary and Benefits

...salary is irrelevant if the job is not a fit for one or both parties. Neither party will know that unless they invest some time in getting to know each other.

— Bill Davis, Negotiation Expert

So you got the call back and a company wants to hire you! Now the dance begins. You now get to set the terms of the relationship.

Negotiation is one of my favorite parts of the hiring process. It's also one most people are uncomfortable with. Negotiating a good salary comes down to information and walk-away. If you can't afford to walk away from an offer, then you'll have a weaker position than someone who can. It's truly amazing how few people are taking advantage of this.

As part of researching this chapter, I interviewed negotiation expert Bill

Davis, who currently teaches at the Wake Forest School of Business in Winston-Salem, NC. When asked about how many job candidates seem to understand and take advantage of their professional value during the salary negotiation, he had this to say:

> That number (percentage) is increasing with all the attention to the need to negotiate salary. However…I'm not sure that many folks do a good job of determining their personal/professional value, nor do they understand the limitations that position[al] value place[s] on what they might be compensated for a particular role in a specific company, industry, location, etc.

I think most people imagine negotiation is an adversarial pursuit with lots of back and forth. Many candidates may just be too shy to push hard, afraid that the company might decide to cut their losses and offer the job to someone else. That's not really true though.

Negotiations don't have to be long, drawn out processes. In one job, I simply declined the initial offer and said they had to come up to a higher number. That was all the conversation I had. In a few days, they countered with $10,000 more. It was all a matter of saying "no" one time to get that much closer to where I wanted to be. Because I was happy with the deal, I took it. It wasn't a hard or painful conversation at all. All I did was reject the initial offer, and that got me a significant bump in my salary. I was able to do that because I had a walk-away, and I researched what I was worth in the market.

A lot of people struggle talking about salary. They think it might make them come off as greedy or money-hungry. We all have bills. Every employer knows you have to pay money for things, and they don't know your personal circumstances (and don't tell them either; your boss doesn't care about your rent or your student loans. They're your problem). Get comfortable talking about your value because that's all recruiters and hiring managers do all day. They talk salary and benefits.

I was actually a lot like that. I didn't want to come off as greedy or money-centric either, but I had bills to pay and a family to support. I looked at it from the idea that I wasn't negotiating for myself so much as for my family. I negotiated a better living for my wife and daughters, and in that I will be fearless.

Remember that you're not just negotiating your livelihood; you're negotiating your earning potential over time. Many companies give raises as a percentage to your base salary. So you want to do everything you can to negotiate a high base, so that your next raise will be higher. That is why you must research what you're worth.

There are tons of great sites like pay.com where you can find out what average salaries are for people with your experience level and education. Use a couple of different sites and average them out. You'll have a good ballpark of what you're worth at that point. Also, if you're a member of a professional organization that publishes annual salaries, be sure to get your hands on that. The Project Management Institute (PMI) publishes an annual salary by experience, education, certifications, and geographic location. Make sure you're looking at the market in the area you're going to work, not where you currently live.

If this job would require you to move, do some research on the cost of living. When I moved from North Carolina to Northern Virginia, I had to absorb a huge cost of living increase. I knew I could not expect to have NC costs with VA wages. Knowing what I needed to make to maintain my family's lifestyle in Northern Virginia was critical information I needed to have. It made my position more powerful because I had the right information.

Finally, when discussing salary, remember that there are other benefits too. For example, are you willing to take less salary for more vacation days? Would you forgo a sign-on bonus for a bump in salary? These are all things you need to consider and prepare for before you begin negotiating. Truthfully, this only really comes up with senior positions. Almost all companies have established benefits options and PTO (paid-time-off) policies. They aren't negotiable because they're standard, but don't assume anything. You can always ask.

Organizing Your Negotiating Points

I recommend putting what you value in a job into a spreadsheet. Having this up front helps clarify what you're comfortable taking, and it allows you the flexibility to accommodate counter offers without losing ground.

Here is a chart to help you organize your thoughts:

Options	Value (-10-10)	Ideal	Walk Away	Initial Offer
Salary	40			
+85K	10	400 (40 x 10)		
+75K	7		280	
65K	-5			
Holidays	5			
Greater than 10	10	50		
6-9	5		25	
PTO	10			
Greater than 25 days	10	100		
18-24 days	8		80	
Fewer than 18 days	-5			

Options	Value (-10-10)	Ideal	Walk Away	Initial Offer
Health Insurance	15			
Fully Covered	10	150		
Discounted	5		75	
None	-10			
Relocation Package	5			
yes	10	50		
no	0		0	
Culture Fit	20			
Great Fit	10	200		
Ok Fit	3		60	
Poor Fit	-10			
Total		950	520	

The chart should look familiar. It's similar to the table you made for what you value in a company. We're just getting more granular now. For the first column, you list the category like Salary or Paid Time Off, and then you list each option underneath. You probably have some different categories in mind, like upward mobility for example. The spreadsheet is meant to be flexible enough that it fits you, but organized so that you can quantify and objectively evaluate several offers.

In the second column, assign a point value to each category. The sum should be 100. Assigning points forces you to list what is most important to you and prioritize. That step is critical. Next, assign a point value to each option underneath each category. Use a scale of negative 10 to positive 10. This means some options can count against the deal (negative), some count for it (positive), and some are neutral (0).

Once that's done, list out the ideal scenario—what you hope to get. This is what you're striving for, so it should be high, yet realistic. You multiply the weight and the value to come up with points. Add all the points up to get your total. Do the same with your walk-away (the point where you are indifferent to taking the job or not).

Now you have something to track against each offer, including your counter-offers. The goal is to end up as close to the ideal as possible, but you would be willing to accept anything above the walk-away. In the example above, you would take anything above 520 points. If an offer is below 520 you walk away. Remember that there's nothing wrong with turning the first offer down. You have to do what is right for you. Do not violate your walk-away. Don't let last-second doubt erode your confidence. If you get less than what you need, you won't be happy and will end up leaving that job within a year most likely.

A lot of times, negotiations won't take place in person: you'll get a phone call. Don't agree to anything right out of the gate, even if the initial offer exceeds your walk-away. You don't have any greater leverage than you have at this moment. The company wants you; they have invested time in you already, and they have a position they need filled. They think you're the person to do it, so confidently make a counter-offer. They won't immediately move on to the next person because you're negotiating. They want you to work for them.

If you're not quick on your feet or the initial offer surprised you, you can request to see everything in writing. You can say something like, "I'm excited you've decided to give me an offer. Would you be able to send it to me in writing?" They're required to give you an official offer letter detailing everything you need to know. If they pressure you then and there to accept, just say, "I'll need to see everything in writing. I can get back to you tomorrow." Buy yourself some time to think about a counter if you need to. If you already know what you'd like to add to the offer, don't be afraid to say so. If they respond with no, you still have a good offer on the table.

Likewise, if they offer you something below your walk-away, feel free to counter immediately. Don't lead them on in thinking you're considering a bad offer. Counter with something you would accept, but make sure it's higher than your minimum. You don't want them to know the lowest you'd accept because that potentially leaves money on the table.

A lot of people have negative fantasies about salary negotiations. By negative fantasy, I mean that they create bad scenarios in their heads that won't happen, and they accept them as truth.

Here's the thing to remember: the company is looking to hire someone competent right away. Companies hire for what they need right now or what they're guaranteed to need real soon. It's rare that there's enough spare budget to hire someone if there's no immediate need.

You are the only one that has the offer at this point for your particular role, so it's in the company's best interest to hire you rather than go back to other candidates who may have taken other jobs at this point. There's a time crunch on their end, and good companies don't want to settle either. They want to hire their first choice because it's so crucial that they find someone competent, capable, culturally compatible, and coachable (didn't think I could come up with that many c-words huh?).

Remember, recruiters deal with this every day, so they aren't surprised if you're willing to negotiate. It's actually a good thing because it means you're paying attention and that you'd probably do well looking out for the company's best interests when dealing with clients.

BATNA (Best Alternative to No Agreement)

The best alternative to no agreement is your fallback plan. It's not the same as your walk-away. Your walk-away should be better than your BATNA because if they're the same, then you're indifferent to taking the new job versus sticking with your current circumstance. One strategy for getting a better deal is to improve your BATNA.

If you already have a job, then that is most likely your BATNA; however, if you don't have a job, you can still work to improve the BATNA. Davis offers some more insight:

...get other offers; don't just look at one potential employer at a time. They [you] need to know what they are worth in the marketplace and, I think, the best way to do that is to look at the annual salary survey data of their professional associations. Don't have any professional memberships? Get them. These are better - more accurate, more persuasive, more objective - than Internet sites. If headhunters are calling you, follow the process long enough to see what the market is doing.

What not to do!! Don't go looking for a job, get an offer, negotiate the offer, and then go to your current firm and tell them that you have another offer - expecting that they will give you a counteroffer, which will serve as your BATNA...If you were to do that to me as your manager, I would wish you well and send you on your way.

Focus on getting more offers before the first negotiation if you can. This is obviously the dream scenario; many companies fighting over you. Even if you get only one other offer though, you can use that to boost your BATNA and your confidence at the negotiation table. Even if you don't hear back, you can send out 10 resumes to competing companies and rightfully say "I'm waiting to hear back on ten other offers."

Another pitfall is comparing your offer with what you currently make. The issue is that the role you're taking may not be the same as the one you're in. Evaluate your offer based on the responsibilities you'd have. If the position is above where you are, you are justified in getting paid fairly for that position.

Remember that negotiations don't have to be adversarial, and when you're negotiating salary it shouldn't be. There are several that are just looking to pay fair wages because they know that you have to work for them after the negotiation. If they press you too hard, you might leave once you realize you're unhappy with your salary and benefits. It doesn't do the company any good to pay you less than market value because you'll leave as soon as another offer comes.

As far as determining your market value, as I said, you can do some research online. That will most likely help you find your positional value; however, there is something more you bring to the company than your role. As Davis points out:

> One wants to determine her personal value – what one brings to the job – from experience, credentials, etc. However, no organization will pay above what a position is worth to them; if they did, they would lose money.

Therefore, if your personal value exceeds your positional value, you'd be overqualified and undercompensated.

So when you're negotiating, remember that the company will not pay more than what the positional value is worth. If you can't take the maximum offer, then you would be better off in a different position. To put it in a clear example, let's say you have an MBA with 5 years' experience as a director of marketing. Your personal value is around $120,000 where you live. You're looking for another job, but the only ones available are for mid-level marketing jobs paying $80,000. No matter how qualified you are, you will not get above $80,000 for that role.

Finally, be confident. If you're more of a naturally nervous person, don't worry about that. The success is in the preparation. Also, don't worry about if you asked for too much money. Your research should show you what your worth. Remember that salary negotiation is the last thing that happens in the hiring process. So at this point, both you and the company have invested a lot of time and consideration. The only time they'll walk away is if you can't reach a deal.

Companies expect you to be competent and diligent. These qualities come through immensely when you spend the time to prepare a well-researched salary negotiation.

Pay Attention to Circumstance

Remember that not everyone can approach a negotiation the same way. People with different circumstances in their lives have different walk-aways. A single person that is out of work may have a much lower threshold than a person who is supported by a working spouse.

When you have a decent walk-away, you can be fairly aggressive with your negotiations. If your walk-away is terrible, it will be harder to stick to your guns. Still, that doesn't mean you have to accept the initial offer. You can always ask for more, and the worst that happens is the company says no. Then you're left with an offer that you can still accept.

Again, if you want to be a good negotiator, there are two things you need: information and a good walk-away. If you can't afford to walk away from the deal, then that limits how hard you can push. If you don't have information on your value in the market place, you're taking shots in the dark. You need to prepare, research what a competitive salary would be, and push for it.

Consider also the size of the company. If you're getting in with a large firm, chances are they have a formalized hiring process with full-time HR staff. They spend a lot of time researching competitive salaries and benefits, and they have a bigger bankroll to pay out money.

Smaller companies are a different story. There's rarely an expansive pool of money to hire talent, so every hire is a critical decision. One bad hire can have huge impacts to a small company, so they have to be hyper judicious. This isn't to say large companies don't scrutinize their applicants, but they have the capital to take more risks.

A small company will probably have someone who functions as a hiring manager but has different primary responsibilities. There are a lot of advantages to working for a small company, but they may not be able to afford a competitive salary for you, and they may not have the most attractive benefits package. This is when your negotiation spreadsheet comes in. You could find a company with an awesome culture, but you'll take a hit in terms of salary and benefits. You have to decide what you're willing to accept.

Finally, you need to be aware of the talent pool in your area. If you're one of a few people with a specific and in-demand skill, you can command a higher salary. That's basic economics (low supply with high demand means higher prices). That being said, just because you have a scarce skill set, doesn't mean you're in demand. You'll have to move to an area where your expertise is needed if you're going to get that higher salary.

Be aware of your market, who is hiring for what, and your value where you live. You can't get an L.A. salary in rural Carolina. Arm yourself with that sort of information, and you'll have a much stronger negotiating position.

Six: Kick Ass in Your First 90 Days

The president of the United States gets 100 days to prove himself; you get 90. The actions you take during your first few months in a new role will largely determine whether you succeed or fail.

—Michael D. Watkins: <u>The First 90 Days</u>

So you got hired! Now begins they honeymoon phase. The first few months can be filled with excitement about learning how to do a new job and getting better acquainted with the awesome company culture. It's also the best time to start building your reputation and earning brownie points in the relationship.

When you build a reputation for success, word will get around quickly. People will find out that you are a hard worker, and you'll have an easier time moving up in the company. That being said, it's easier to come in and start building that type of reputation rather than trying to claw your way out of a bad first impression.

When you start a job, nobody is expecting you to be immediately good at everything. Even if your role is something you've done before, you won't know the culture of the company, and you won't know the people yet. You don't want to come in and start making arbitrary decisions just to make it seem like you know what you're doing. First of all, it's not likely to be received well by your colleagues or direct reports if you're at that level. Take time to learn the way things work at your new company. Even so, don't be afraid to draw from past experience and offer suggestions; just do so with humility. Your delivery is everything in cases like this. You want to come across as helpful but open to suggestion. Something like, "I've seen something like this before, and that time we did it this way. It seemed to work well there. Maybe it could work here, unless there's something I'm not aware of." Now you've offered helpful advice but admitted that there are circumstances you're not aware of. Even if someone explains why your suggestion won't work, you've at least shown you're a thoughtful contributor.

Results are big in the first 90 days. Find and go after small wins. A lot of times when you start some place new, you'll have some down time as you get ramped up to your responsibilities. If you see something that could use improvement that you know you can do, go ahead and do it or offer to do it. For example, if you notice that a file structure is really frustrating or confusing on a team's project, see if you can find a way to better organize it. That sort of work is easy to accomplish and builds you a good reputation.

Once you become fully immersed in your job, your time will get monopolized doing other things. If you've already had a few wins, people will continue to think positively of you even when your opportunities of going above and beyond are further between. That's why it's so important to make sure your first few months are successful ones.

Another thing you can do is be sure to call out when others are doing a good job. When you create an atmosphere of support and encouragement, people will notice, and you'll be praised for it too.

Mentorship

The best thing you can do is to seek out a mentor. Your company may have an official mentorship program where you have one assigned. That's good if your company does that. Your mentor is there to help you and probably knows a bit about the work you're supposed to be doing. Depending on the corporate culture, you may feel completely comfortable talking to your mentor about anything, but if you aren't, you can try to find one in a different department. There's nothing wrong with having an unofficial mentor. Find someone familiar with the company, but far enough removed to where you can air your concerns without fear of word getting around. You want honest help.

Make a point to go to lunch with people. Establish friendships as best you can at all levels of the company. Take your boss out to lunch one day. Find influential people in the company and go to lunch with them, even if they aren't your boss. Take out your direct reports a few times. The more people you know and the more connected you are, the better reputation you can have. You might also get some sage advice, and you can help others as well.

It's incredible how rarely people take that initiative to network within their own company. I know it's harder for some than it is for others. There are people who seem to be social butterflies while others might have anxiety about that kind of situation. Do your best to make friends and meet new people within the company. Even if you have to take it slow, it's better than not doing it at all. I'm not saying you have to schmooze and play golf with the CEO (though if you can and you like that sort of thing, go right ahead). Just make an honest effort to reach out to people and expand your network. Start off by asking for advice. People are flattered and feel respected if you ask their opinions. They're pretty likely to open up to you. Then try to use their advice, even if it's just a part of it. A lot of times, you'll get some pretty good tips.

When you know people in the company and have a good reputation, you are first in line for good projects and promotions. Those sorts of things go to people that can be trusted to do a job well. The only way people know you do good work is if you do good work and they know you.

Attitude

Having the right attitude will do wonders for your career. People with the right attitude learn more, they get along better with teammates, and they get more work done. Whenever I'm picking people for my project teams, I'll more often favor someone with fewer skills and a better attitude than someone with better skills and a bad attitude.

The right attitude is not being a yes-person, and it's also not about shooting down ideas without offering anything in return. Having the right attitude is about seeing opportunity in everything. Recognize that failure is the first step to success. Understand that just because you don't know something now doesn't mean you can't learn it. Having the right attitude is about being patient with teammates, being willing to help, and knowing how and when to say no.

You never want to come off as condescending to someone. In the business world, you deal with a lot of different personalities and a lot of different skill sets. You may very well work for someone that knows less about what you do than you do. It happens quite a bit in the IT world. If you're technical, you might wind up with a boss that's not. On the other hand, you may know more about business or have better people skills than someone else you work with. Be patient with others and recognize that you may have vastly different strengths. Don't dismiss them simply because they have a hard time with something that comes naturally to you.

Still, you will come across the occasional jerk. Hopefully it doesn't turn out to be your boss, but it does happen. There are some cases where bosses are threatened by their high performing employees. I've been fortunate enough not to have experienced this personally, but I know people that have. Those sorts of bosses tend to say bad things about you or try to sabotage you. It sucks, but be wary. In those situations, if you've networked well and proven yourself to other influential people in the company, they will figure out what's going on.

Building Rapport

As a new hire, you want to build a rapport with people. This includes people above you, at your level, and below you. If you happen to be a manager, remember that people will work harder when they know you care about their wellbeing. That means showing appreciation for their work. Knowing a lot of people at your level opens up ways for you to seek advice from others that know the company and can relate to your job. Making yourself known to people above you means that you're visible and will get noticed when you do your job well.

Here are a few simple things you can do to build rapport:

1. Randomly bring in donuts. Most everyone likes donuts. If you find some people that don't, find out what they like and bring it in for them. It shows that you're thoughtful, and people love the donut person.

2. Ask for advice. Try to do it in a private setting. I usually like to invite people out to lunch. It's less formal, gets you away from the office, but allows you to establish a connection. Asking for advice does two things for you: you learn important information, and people see that you are a self-initiating self-improver. Both are good things; however, only ask advice if you genuinely want it. Asking too many people their opinions and ignoring all of them will backfire.

3. Call out when a colleague goes above and beyond their job. Show appreciation for what they did. This is especially important for co-workers and people that report to you. You can praise your

boss too, but doing it too much will come off like you're sucking up, and your co-workers won't like that.

4. Pitch in to help others when they're struggling. Helping other people out will immediately make you valuable, plus you get to learn a little bit more about company operations, which will help you perform your job better. Only offer to help when you actually can. You don't want to be the person that says they'll help and then actually doesn't.

If you'd like more strategies on what you can do to be successful in the first 90 days, I recommend reading <u>The First 90 Days</u> by Michael D. Watkins. That book goes into quite a bit of depth and offers some interesting anecdotes for you to consider.

Do everything you can to kick ass in your first three months. This is the start of your reputation, and you want to make it a good one. You also want to start bringing value to the company as soon as possible. New hires lose the company money because they're not at full productivity yet. The company is paying more to the new hire in salary and benefits than they are receiving in billable work. On average, at 90 days an employee should be contributing at least as much as they're costing. The harder you work to bring value sooner, the better your reputation and the more likely your success.

Conclusion

Thanks for reading my book. I hope you've found something valuable to take with you on your job hunt.

By now, you are better prepared to craft a great resume and knock your interview out of the park. Then, you can negotiate a higher salary like the badass you are.

Be sure to visit my websites: austinfadely.com and collegeconquerors.com for some useful tools you can download for free and use. I also host resume writing and negotiation webinars.

If you have any thoughts or ideas about this subject, I'd love to hear from you.

Email me at the address below, follow my Facebook page, or send me a Tweet @austinfadely.

-Austin Fadely

austin@collegeconquerors.com

http://austinfadely.com

http://collegeconquerors.com

https://www.facebook.com/afadely

https://www.facebook.com/collegeconquerors

Interviews

Through the course of writing this book, I interviewed several people from different functional roles. The interviews are organized by role so that you can gain a better sense of what a recruiter might be looking for versus a hiring manager. Each interview serves a purpose. A phone screen for example, might just be trying to assess if your experience matches your resume. If you pass that, then you'd come to an in-person interview, where you'll be more evaluated on cultural fit. You may also have a technical interview with someone that can dig deeper into your skill set.

There are several overarching and consistent themes, which we've covered in the book; however, each interview you have is with a person, who has their own experience, frame of reference, and pet peeves. Some will have more experience interviewing while some have less. Some may be formally trained to conduct interviews while others aren't.

I've included transcripts to emphasize the variety of responses and the human element of the hiring process.

Recruiters

Michael Bacchus — Director of Recruiting (Consulting Firm)

How long have you been a recruiter?

> Since 1998

Roughly how many people have you interviewed during that time?

> Thousands

What platforms do you use mainly to search for candidates?

> I start with employee referrals, and people our employees know. Networking is key when you're looking for a job. Get involved with user groups and likeminded people. Even if it's not directly related to what you're doing, networking is still the most effective way for us to find candidates.
>
> Then you get into LinkedIn/Social platforms. LinkedIn is the leader.
>
> Then there are job boards, but they aren't as fertile ground as they used to be. Recruiters have become much more sophisticated, and the job boards tend to have the b-level candidates. That's a broad generalization; there are still great candidates on the job boards by accident (old or abandoned profiles). Some of the job boards have gotten pretty good at interacting with LinkedIn because content is fresher there.

How do you search for candidates? Are there any common keywords you search for or is it specific to the job you're trying to fill?

> I always start as specific as possible. Every keyword and attribute that matches what I'm looking for. If I find one or two diamonds (that match everything), great! Then I widen scope out from there. More often than not, you can find the diamond, but the problem is that they may not be available or we may not be able to afford them.

Do you think people that post resumes to job sites stand a good chance of being found even if they don't apply for jobs specifically?

> Yes, if you make yourself open enough, like on Monster. If you're open to relocation, will live anywhere, and have a broadly SEO-optimized resume with a lot of different keywords searches, you can be found. The problem is that you'll be so general that recruiters will wonder if you would be a good fit. So it's best to have a resume that is optimized to be found but also targeted to what you're looking for. However, you don't want to be too specific with your keywords unless you just want that one job. If you're open to different positions, don't go so narrow in your keywords or else you won't find that job. E.g.: work in Ashburn, with x benefits, and y salary.

If/When would you approach potential candidates that haven't specifically applied to your job post?

We approach them all the time. We look for job fit first, regardless of source. It all happens concurrently: job board, LinkedIn, and networking. We're constantly combing all those various sources. We are looking for candidates that are a match first and are available second.

What factors do you consider before you reach out to a potential candidate?

Resume lending itself to potential fit.

Do you do any additional research on a candidate before you call? If so, what do you research and what are you looking for?

Typically we do some research beforehand. We hit LinkedIn and do a Google search. Google is surprisingly good at uncovering little gems about people. It can lead to recruiters finding your Facebook page. I've heard of recruiters doing a Google search and finding a candidate's Facebook profile. Then that person makes an ass of themselves over the weekend and doesn't get the job. It might call into question their judgment. As we get deeper into the social media world, as connected as they are, it's going to become more challenging for candidates to have a clean social media presence because 10-12 year old kids don't understand that. Some 22 year-olds don't understand that.

What are you looking for in the phone interview?

Conversation: the ability to have a two-way, interesting

conversation. By interesting, we are going to cover some nuts and bolts. I'm trying to determine fit. If they aren't looking for fit, I wonder at their level of interest. The exception would be a cold-call where they may not be looking. That two-way conversational skill is what will put someone over the top.

Are there any common mistakes people can avoid?

If I'm catching them out of the blue, I'm a lot more lenient. If we have a scheduled call, and they don't know anything about me or my company, then they probably haven't taken the conversation seriously. With access to information, they should at least have an awareness of the company and be prepared for the interview. If I do catch someone unprepared, and they can handle the conversation with ease, all the better.

Are there any pet peeves you have that you've encountered on a phone interview?

Not really, people have different idiosyncrasies, speech cadences, accents. None of that bothers me. There was an interview I had where the guy was yelling at his kids while he was interviewing. He wasn't trying to escape them to have the interview. He was having multiple conversations at the same time and yelling at his kids. He kept trying to carry on the conversation, which wasn't fine. He wasn't dedicating his full attention to the interview.

What's the most common reason a potential candidate doesn't proceed to the next level?

The most common reason is that they're not a fit skill-set wise. That or candidate timing, i.e.: they're not available or not available at the moment to take a new job.

What are some of the major character traits you look for?

Examples of integrity, honesty, self-awareness, like understanding their strengths and weaknesses. I've had people tell me their weakness is that they work too hard. That shows someone has learned how to interview, and it's just silly. When I get a canned answer, I like to dig a little deeper to get under that. Is it just a case of nerves? What's behind the canned answer will tell me if they've prepared, if they're nervous, what do they really have to say? Sometimes it makes them uncomfortable, and that tells me they might be trying to hide something, so I poke a little bit more. Candidates need to be comfortable asking the follow up question to go deeper. I think some interviewers stay a little too surface level and never get to a deeper understanding and appreciation from where someone is coming from. Granted you're in a compressed timeframe, but you need to connect with someone to find what their drivers are, and what we have to offer to marry that together.

Any pet peeves in the in-person interview?

Lack of preparation, lack of understanding, and lack of awareness. They don't know anything about the company or the role. Lack of awareness gets into the art of conversation and social cues. It's really the art of conversation. You take into consideration external influences or conditions that could cause people to have different feelings. All things being equal, if they're unaware of how the conversation is flowing, it's not a good sign for a fit, especially for a consulting/client facing environment.

Please explain your company's hiring philosophy.

> We look for exceptional people. The roles that we interview people for, the interviewers have typically done those roles and understand what it is the candidates will be doing. We can have very good conversations and good interviews to see if someone is going to be a fit for the role, for the team, for the culture. We'll take less skill, be it technical or functional, if someone's a great cultural fit and a strong consulting fit. We look for flexibility and a desire to learn and grow. We look for diversity, not robots— not just culturally but different schools of thought. I want diversity of thought and experience because that brings a very rich background to create solutions that are meaningful to clients.

Is there any other advice you would like to offer my readers?

> From a hiring manager perspective; they need to be comfortable in a conversation. Know the audience; be able to read the cues. Don't change who you are, but understand the situation and mold your conversation to match the occasion. That goes for people that are technical as well as functional.

Interview published with permission from Michael Bacchus. Transcribed from in-person interview, 5/29/2015.

John Hill — Former Recruiter in Staffing and IT (Placement Agency)

How long have you been a recruiter?

> I have 12 years recruiting with 8 years IT.

Roughly how many people have you interviewed during that time?

> About one thousand

What platforms do you use mainly to search for candidates?

> I use a lot of online job boards like dice, monster, hotjobs, LinkedIn, local job boards, and industry-specific job boards. Everything is online now a days. I used to run ads in papers and online papers, but the majority is online, social media, liked LinkedIn, or posting jobs to job boards.

How do you search for candidates?

> For hard to find ones, you've got to search for them. I do keyword searching, Boolean searching – use parentheses or stars, but you can break it down further for a more granular search, It's a format where you can hone in your keyword searching. For example, I can't put in JDEdwards because I might get people back with the name Edward. Keywords typically revolve around the skill set.

> In my opinion, you can't overdo your resume. Put in keywords

for stuff that you've done. Don't just put Word, put in Microsoft Word. Don't put Office, put Microsoft Excel, Microsoft Sharepoint, etc. Be specific. Be very specific with the skills; otherwise, I might not find you in the keyword search.

A lot of people don't have experience with the way recruiters are looking for people now a days.

Do you think people that post resumes to job sites stand a good chance of being found even if they don't apply for jobs specifically?

Yea, I do. I think it's good to do both, but if they're actively looking, they need to be looking for jobs and applying for them. Sometimes it's a pain, and it takes time, but I think it's necessary if you're really looking. You need to take the time to do that.

If you're just kind of looking, then you can just put your resume on there [a job board] and not have to apply.

I always say that looking for a job is a full time job. You need to get up every day and spend the time actively looking. You need to spend the time because you're one of millions looking.

If/When would you approach potential candidates that haven't specifically applied to your job post?

If I'm looking at their resume and see a resume that seems like a good fit, I'll reach out. I go by the 60/70% rule. Nobody is going to be a 100% match for what I'm looking for. If I think they'll be a good fit, I go ahead and call or email them. The worst thing is that they say no. Even if they aren't interested, use that opportunity to network to find others within the industry/degree field that may be looking.

What factors do you consider before you reach out to a potential candidate?

You want to look local first, except for people that note that they will relocate. It's pointless to find someone perfect but they live somewhere else. What are the odds they'll move here? Not likely. You start local, and then you go skill wise and degree. Look for the right education/skills combination. Then you reach out to them. Start real focused, and if you don't find anything, spread out.

I might have to widen the search and look for people with more experience or less experience.

Do you do any additional research on a candidate before you call? If so, what do you research and what are you looking for?

I look at the resume. There have been times where I'll look and see if they have a social media presence. Maybe not before I call initially, but once it seems like they may be a fit, I'll see what they're LinkedIn looks like.

Once they get to the interview process, I'll look more at their Facebook and other social media. I've had managers that as soon as they see a name will see if the candidate has Facebook,

LinkedIn, or Twitter. I think it's becoming more and more that people are doing that.

They need to have a professional email address. You need to put like JenniferJones7742@yahoo.com. I know of managers that have turned candidates down based on the email address. A lot of people are looking, so you can be picky on candidates.

Make sure your voicemail message is professional. You don't need music playing or anything. Just have your name. Companies will pay attention to that. Have it set up. It's absolutely annoying to try to call a candidate and they don't have their voicemail set up. You're looking for a job; you're missing an opportunity. They may call and skip and go on to the next person.

As for social media stuff: where are you, and what are you putting on there? More and more people are looking at Twitter, Facebook, and Instagram just to see what kind of person you are. What are you in to, what are your hobbies? You need to take all that into consideration when you're looking for a job.

What are you looking for in the phone interview?

I'm trying to get a feel for them. I think as a recruiter, you want to do as much listening as you do talking. I'll get a feel for the person and ask them stuff on their resume to see if they answer it the same way. Do they really know what they're talking about? If their resume and LinkedIn matches what they tell me, then it's more believable. I might drill down on a project they mentioned.

It's not about what their team did, but what did that person specifically do?

I'm asking questions based on the resume, experience, and degree. Why are they interested in this area? If they applied to the job, I want to know what they know about the company because they should do their research. If I'm randomly calling them, they should still know something about the company once the interview comes up.

I can't ask questions that are too personal, but I can ask about their ability to relocate; however, if you throw personal stuff out in the call, I'll take it.

I do some personality questions as well, but the goal for me as a recruiter is to make sure they're a match for the company. Once they get to a hiring manager, the manager may break the interview down more and look for personality fit. As a recruiter, I'm more skill based.

Are there any common mistakes people can avoid?

Don't answer anything in an interview as yes/no. I don't think you ever answer no. If you haven't done something, offer something that's similar and relevant that you did do. If you don't know a skill, don't lie about it, but offer up examples of where you're improving. You don't want to go on too long, but be specific with how you have used a skill if you have done it. Elaborate, but don't be too long. Don't answer just yes or no.

Don't let the recruiter ask all the questions. Have three or four questions based on the job description and the company. If it's a recruiter calling out of the blue, you may not need all the questions, but if it's a prepared interview, then you need to be prepared with questions and know a bit about the company. Do some research. Having good questions shows you're interested in the opportunity and the company.

Are there any pet peeves you have that you've encountered on a phone interview?

People not elaborating. When you ask "what company is this again/what job is this again?" when the call is scheduled, that bothers me.

What's the most common reason a potential candidate doesn't proceed to the next level?

The most common reasons are that they are not a match personality-wise or skill-set wise. If might also be if they're more experienced it may not be a good fit money-wise. Basically the recruiter doesn't feel they're a match.

Please explain your company's hiring philosophy.

As a recruiter, you learn the company, the manager, and the team. You learn as much as you can, and then you use every avenue possible to locate the right candidate and the right match. You can't just try one, two, or three things and give up.

It's got to be a match on both sides. Both the company and the candidate need to be equally interested and find that right match.

Is there any other advice you would like to offer my readers?

It's a hard job, but put in the time and effort and get your name out there. I think for professionals, one of the key things is using the right professional and social media outlets. LinkedIn is a major outlet now. Take the time to learn and use LinkedIn right. Recommendations are very important on there. Try to have a few recommendations for each job. Networking is very important if you're looking for a job. Get on LinkedIn, get connected to your friends, and connect with their friends. If you're not online, you're behind the game.

Interview published with permission from John Hill. Transcribed from phone interview, 6/30/2015.

Rachel Neuschaefer — Senior Recruiting Consultant (Consulting Firm)

How long have you been a recruiter?

> Since September 2002. I've done staffing and managed Campus recruiting.

Roughly how many people have you interviewed during that time?

> I guess hundreds.

What platforms do you use mainly to search for candidates?

> LinkedIn is the number one tool.

> Employee referrals play a big role. Best way in is to know somebody on the inside.

> I do a lot of searches on indeed.com

> Networking events and career fairs sometimes. User groups like on meetup.com.

> I use Dice, but I have not had as much success on there as with LinkedIn.

> I started using Twitter, but I haven't had much success.

> As a recruiter, I'm always open to new approaches to meet people. I attended a conference and learned about setting up groups on Facebook for head-hunting.

How do you search for candidates? Are there any common keywords you search for or is it specific to the job you're trying to fill?

Keywords are specific for the job. There may be some common industry terms. I start off with broad search terms and see what the results may be. Then I work down to specific keywords. I will look into second and third degree contacts on people that match the skill set. Recruiter accounts on LinkedIn can see every profile on LinkedIn.

Do you think people that post resumes to job sites stand a good chance of being found even if they don't apply for jobs specifically?

Yes, but only if they post to Monster or Dice. Unspoken recruiter rule is that the most qualified candidates are not openly posting. Talented people tend to be passively looking or are already employed. When people are looking for something, they reach out to their network, and it snowballs from there.

One time, my company made me take a 30% pay cut and work more hours. I Googled the top 25 tech companies in the area. I connected with somebody from every single company and then sent an email marketing myself. Then, I called around to those companies once I connected with people on LinkedIn. Candidates need to learn to sell themselves.

If/When would you approach potential candidates that haven't specifically applied to your job post?

I would reach out the second I find them. If I see a candidate that could be a fit, it's worth a conversation. What comes out of that conversation determines the next step.

What factors do you consider before you reach out to a potential candidate?

Typos on the resume is huge. Some managers won't talk to a candidate with typos in the resume. Consider the resume as marketing you. The only possible exception is if English is your second language but the skill set is right. Even then, have someone review your resume to make sure it is correct. I've seen candidates where the first line on their resume has a typo.

Do you do any additional research on a candidate before you call? If so, what do you research and what are you looking for?

No. Recruiters look at your resume for four to five seconds. We work in volume to fill a funnel. If we can identify someone within the company that knew you at an old company, we would talk to that person. Otherwise, we don't really have time to research until an offer is given.

What are you looking for in the phone interview? Are there any common mistakes people can avoid?

Typically I'm looking for a skill set match. Do you have the skills necessary to do the job? Back up your claims with specific examples.

Beyond that, I look for communication skills and social interaction. There are candidates who culturally have a different way of dealing with recruiters. I'm trying to capture information: why did you leave your last job? What are you looking to do? What are you looking to make? Once you give your salary requirements, you don't need to list reasons why. If you start justifying your salary requirement, you could shoot yourself in the foot.

One of my biggest pet peeves is when you justify your salary requirements. Everyone sounds nervous about their salary requirement. Nobody is comfortable talking about it, but I just need an answer. If there is a question about your salary requirement, I will ask you. Normally, I will ask what you made before. Some companies require it. If you are underpaid, that is a valid reason for leaving a company, but you're probably not going to get a $50,000 increase in your next job. Another question I have if you were underpaid, why did you wait so long to leave?

Even if you refuse to say what your last salary was, a recruiter can find out. We can verify it during the background investigation. We can verify your most recent salary. We are legally allowed to see tax forms if there is any doubt about what you were making before.

If your skill set lines up with someone else, you may get more money based on what that other person made. There are a lot of behind the scenes stuff. Recruiting is a fast paced position, and it's frustrating.

A question I get a lot from candidates is "how soon can I follow up after an interview?" That's a good thing to ask. You can ask 10 recruiters the same questions and get 10 different answers.

I love an objective on a resume. Many newer recruiters don't like to see it. Most recruiters don't read cover letters. If you're a coder, you better be on Git-hub and Stack Overflow. The best developers are active. Be active in whatever community you're a part of. This goes back to personal branding and how you are different from anyone else who's applied for this job.

Are there any pet peeves you have that you've encountered on a phone interview?

Salary justification really does annoy me.

It's frustrating when candidates go on tangents and forget to answer the question. Asking a question twice is annoying.

Name dropping is a double edge sword. It can be annoying, but if you drop the CEO's name, I'll listen.

[Another pet peeve is] when candidates are really specific about the title. Titles are different across companies.

What's the most common reason a potential candidate doesn't proceed to the next level?

No skill set match, or the resume doesn't match the real work.

Some companies do assessments; you need to pass them to proceed.

[During the interview] say your answer, and shut your mouth. Candidates tend to trail off in concerning things. One candidate shared a story that led the interviewer to believe the person wasn't ethical and lacked integrity.

Please explain your company's hiring philosophy.

Profile Hires – typically, what we are looking for is the social/cultural fit. You know it when you feed it. Everybody has a shared cultural trait. For a profile fit, we look for natural problem solvers. They're very bright; they're flexible; they're hard working, and they've had jobs that prove all these for the most part. Flexible, bright, hard-working.

Is there any other advice you would like to offer my readers?

Sell yourself, and don't be afraid to connect with people on LinkedIn. That's the best way. Look for the recruiters, CTOs, director of HR. Connect with them and send them an email. You'll almost always get a response. It's a skill you may have to find.

Ask recruiter for specific feedback. They want you to feel you want to work here. Nobody wants to hire a 5th choice.

[One of the] biggest complaint against recruiters is not hearing back in a timely manner, but if you're getting the job, you'll probably hear back soon.

Recruiters can ask whatever they want, but most of the time they just verify dates of employment.

Working for a big name company may make you more attractive to recruiters.

As for resumes, generally it's one page per 10 years. I recommend having an expanded resume and a condensed resume.

Interview published with permission from Rachel Neuschaefer. Transcribed from in-person interview, 5/27/2015.

Kristen Spivey — IT Recruiter (Placement Agency)

How long have you been a recruiter?

> 5 years

Roughly how many people have you interviewed during that time?

> Gosh there are so many. I normally try to have 5 face to face interviews per week but if phone conversations (profiles) count then that number is really large. I profile approximately 5 people per day, sometimes more.

What platforms do you use mainly to search for candidates?

> CareerBuilder and LinkedIn.

How do you search for candidates?

> I utilize Boolean search strings.

Do you think people that post resumes to job sites stand a good chance of being found even if they don't apply for jobs specifically?

> Yes, for smaller not well known companies it is hard to get people to apply directly to the posting so recruiter will often do searches on the boards.

If/When would you approach potential candidates that haven't specifically applied to your job post?

> Daily. It is expensive to post positions on large job boards so a

lot of candidates come from job board searches.

What factors do you consider before you reach out to a potential candidate?

Skill set, longevity, and location.

Do you do any additional research on a candidate before you call? If so, what do you research and what are you looking for?

Not before I call. After I call I will search LinkedIn for their profile to connect with them.

What are you looking for in the phone interview?

Solid communication skills, easy of explanation of their experience and skill set.

Are there any common mistakes people can avoid?

Speaking quickly and assuming the person on the other end knows as much about that type of work as they do.

Are there any pet peeves you have that you've encountered on a phone interview?

Trying to rush the conversation, background noise, rude, quick speaking, chewing on the phone, ring back tones and no voicemail set up.

What's the most common reason a potential candidate doesn't proceed to the next level?

Lack of relevant experience.

Please explain your company's hiring philosophy.

We present candidates that possess the right skill, experience level, longevity and that have good reference checks.

Is there any other advice you would like to offer my readers?

Do not lie about your experience or dates of employment. Be yourself, be confident in your ability to perform the job and learn new skill sets.

Interview published with permission from Kristen Spivey. Email interview, 8/8/2015.

Hiring Managers

Chris Casini — Territory Manager (National Beverage Distributor)

How long have you been conducting professional interviews?

2 years

Roughly how many people have you interviewed during that time?

50

What are the major character traits you look for in an interviewee?

Confident, outgoing, friendly, and assertive.

I like interviewees that ask good questions of the job or the company. Asking a question and displaying knowledge of the job and company shows initiative. I like it when candidates ask about the interviewer or ask about the career path the interviewer took to get to where he or she is.

Don't ask about pay. Don't ask about benefits. When the job is offered to you, that's when you analyze the pay and benefits. During the interview is not the time to ask that.

Are there any pet peeves you have that you've seen in an interview?

I've interviewed a number of senior-level people, and they're ready to enter the workforce and be professional. What I've noticed is that the entry-level ones that have no experiences in college or organizations, whether sports, fraternity, or some type of club, don't have a lot to offer in the interview. 80% of the beef in an interview are the experiences you have to draw on to answer the questions. If you don't do anything in college other than lifeguard over the summer, you'll struggle in the interview.

Getting a 4.0 without joining organizations or contributing in other ways won't help. A lot of times you'll take a question and relate it to an experience in one of your organizations, and being able to talk about the situation and how you dealt with it is very valuable.

Interview published with permission from Chris Casini. Transcribed from phone interview, 4/26/2011.

Morgan Foley — Managing Director (Consulting Firm)

How long have you been conducting professional interviews?

> 16 years

Roughly how many people have you interviewed during that time?

> A couple hundred

What are the major character traits you look for in an interviewee?

> Confidence and trustworthiness are the top two personality traits. I do more soft skills now that I'm advanced in my career, but I still do technical questions to determine skill set fit.

What sort of research do you do on your interviewees before or after the interview? Google? Facebook?

> Honestly, I read through the resume. I don't do any stalking of sorts. I assume that other people are doing that. Part of it is age and generation. When I first starting hiring, Facebook and Google didn't exist. I also feel that people can be very different in their personal and professional lives, and I'm evaluating them for professional life. I will glance here and there on LinkedIn. Most of that is to see if I know anyone they know or see where they've worked before. I might use those folks as an informal reference.

Are there any pet peeves you have that you've seen in an interview?

> Not dressed formally like more casual shirts. Also, I don't like it

when people get too casual in their conversations. I like to get people out of the formal question and answering phase, but at the same time I don't want people to think I'm their buddy, and they start swearing. For some, it's the slip of the tongue, for others they're just too casual. So it's just general inappropriateness.

There are lots of people that don't have the skill sets they advertise. When you ask them to start describing what they did, and all they can do is repeat the bullet points on their resume, that's a key indicator that they don't understand what they said they do.

What's the goal you have in mind when interviewing a candidate?

For me it's to figure out their capacity to learn, think on their feet, and culture fit. I look at internal culture fit for the company and also the ability to fit and adapt culturally to our clients.

Are their common interview mistakes people can avoid?

I think really what people tend to do is forget that when they're interviewing, it's not just a company interviewing them; they should be interviewing the company. When I ask if the interviewee has questions, a lot of times I get questions that aren't substantial or substantive. That's the time for the interviewee to ask questions about the company and see if it's a good fit that aligns with what they want.

What is the most common reason a candidate won't proceed to the next step?

Generally, it's failing to make that positive impression. It can also be a failure to show confidence or appearing too cocky. It could be a failure to interact well and adapt to situations. I've interviewed people that are very technically competent, but you can't get them to engage. At that point, I don't care how skilled you are, I don't want to work with you.

Please explain your company's hiring philosophy.

Overall, people take the approach of: "Do I want this person on my team." It might not be about what you know today, but how resourceful you are and how much leadership potential you have. That's really what we want to look for. A lot of times, it's soft skills in a lot of situations.

Any other advice?

Research the company that you're interviewing for. It's more than research the website. See if you know people there and talk to them about their experiences. Really take the time in the interview process to connect with the person that's interviewing you. Take the opportunity to truly figure out if the company is a good match for you.

Interview published with permission from Morgan Foley. Transcribed from phone interview, 6/24/2015.

Justin Klingman — Former Manager, Web Software Development & Functioning Hiring Manager (Web Development & Marketing Company)

How long have you been conducting professional interviews?

> 5 years

Roughly how many people have you interviewed during that time?

> 50

What are the major character traits you look for in an interviewee?

> I look for honesty number one. I feel like I'm good if I'm figuring out whether they're telling the truth or not. I look at professionalism. Some people aren't professional at all. I look for some shred of professionalism. If I write you a somewhat formal email about an interview, and you respond, "Sure, sounds good," that looks bad to me. Hard working is another thing I look for. I look for those who have the dedication to see the project through whether it took overtime or not. I need people you don't have to beg or entice with something to see them take ownership and have the dedication to the project.

What sort of research do you do on your interviewees before or after the interview? Google? Facebook?

> I would look online. I would look them up on Google to see if I could find past projects, blogs, or news articles on a company

website. For the portfolios, I would look at the sites they included to see if they seem to know what they were doing. I also went to social media. I wanted to see Facebook posts and Instagram pictures. I wanted to know if they presented themselves like a screw up or a professional. Some people I saw were badmouthing their companies or clients, which isn't a good thing to do. If I found a good amount of information, I'd compare it against the resume or LinkedIn. What kind of projects did they work on? What kind of feedback they were getting? I don't believe in references really because they [the candidates] would include only people that would give them a glowing review. It may not have always been the whole picture.

Are there any pet peeves you have that you've seen in an interview?

The number one thing is the professionalism. It starts out with the responses to the initial inquiry. Show some shred of professionalism. I'm not expecting hyper formal, but some sort of professional response. That is a huge pet peeve of mine. It also depends on the company. If you're applying to some fun, extremely laid-back company, you might be able to be more informal, but if you don't know then just assume a professional manner.

The second thing is not being prepared for the interview. I spoke with one person that bashed a technology we supported even though the logo for that product was right on the website. On the other hand, if they could name some specifics about the company, then that showed they did some research. Preparing for the interview and knowing something about the company, what they do, what technologies they use; it's all stuff they could find out on the public site. Lack of professionalism and preparedness are the top pet peeves, and lying is a big pet peeve.

What's the goal you have in mind when interviewing a candidate?

I want the best person for the job—someone we're not going to waste time and money on. At a small company, you can't really miss. It's a lot of time to onboard somebody, and there's not that many others that can mentor. The goal is that you find somebody that you don't have to mentor as much. You want that match for the skills and technologies you're looking for. You don't want to train the person on things that they should know already. In the case of a developer, you don't want to train them how to be a developer, but you will invest time getting that person onboarded. I want to find the person that I could trust could be helpful quickly.

I typically ask people how they learned things because at a small company, we needed people that could learn on their own.

Are their common interview mistakes people can avoid?

Embellishing what you know. Don't say you know something when you don't. Just because you read about something but have never applied it—that is not a reason to put it on your resume as something you know. Do not oversell yourself because you will get exposed eventually.

Another mistake is just not being professional. They show up late, or in jeans, without copies of the resume, a notebook, and a pen. Be prepared to take notes or fill out forms. Some people walked in with polo shirts, khakis, and nothing in their hands.

What is the most common reason a candidate won't proceed to the next step?

I think it's if the level of skillset doesn't match what they say. In development, it's so easy to say you have a skill when you open a resume and see what code languages they know, but when it becomes apparent in the interview that their level of skill doesn't match the resume, they don't get pushed on to the next step.

Please explain your company's hiring philosophy?

Typically at a small company, there's not as much time invested in it. We did the phone interview, and the in-person interview, and then we would make a decision. There were some exceptions, but for the most part, the process was those two interviews.

We tried to look for people that fit our culture and company lifestyle. We wanted people that were team players.

Is there any other advice you would offer a potential candidate?

I think one thing that I always liked in an interviewee is seeing if they follow the lead of the person interviewing. If they're serious and formal, be more formal. If the interviewer is being more relaxed and laid back, follow that lead, but don't push it too far. It's not up to you to dictate the interview; it's up to the person interviewing you. Follow their lead.

Also, keep your answers concise. Say what you need to say succinctly. Don't ramble on. Don't show up late, and don't show up too early. Sometimes, we're not ready for you.

Interview published with permission from Justin Klingman. Transcribed from phone interview, 7/19/2015.

Tarun Kundhi — Vice President/CTO (Commercial Printer)

How long have you been conducting professional interviews?

15 years

Roughly how many people have you interviewed during that time?

100 across four companies, had to hire 20 people

Are there ways interviewees can ask engaging questions from their interviewer?

It might be difficult to determine what the position you're applying for does. A lot of companies will use a title, but it may not reflect what it does at all. For example, a staff accountant is different from one company to the next. The interviewee needs to take the time to find out what the company does, then you can ask questions about the job and how it relates to what the company does. In this day and age, it's much easier to find out what a company does than it's ever been.

Google is your friend. Go to the company's web page, and try to figure out who their competitors are. That will tell you a lot about who they are and what they do. Also, spend a little time finding out about the person who's going to interview you.

You should ask how you'd be evaluated. How are expectations laid out? Let's say there are two opportunities you're exploring. One may seem great, and it's with a start-up, but they have no clue how to answer the question. Then you'll have another one that's good or similar, but the company is more established and has concrete rules. The only way you'll get promoted and proceed is if you are successful, and you can only do that if you and your boss are on the same page about what the expectations are. It doesn't matter if you're working for the biggest jerk in the world: you are more likely to succeed if you are exceeding expectations. It can help you determine which job is right for you, and it also allows you to evaluate if what the hiring manager said is reality.

What are the major character traits you look for in an interviewee?

Punctual, professional, articulate, and the rest will vary based upon the position. I do believe that psycho analysis has validity, and I do believe and utilize tools that will profile people (like Meyers-Briggs), which are only relevant if you profile the job first. Those tools should be used by an interviewer, but not in isolation. It should never be used as the only criteria.

What sort of research do you do on your interviewees before or after the interview? Google? Facebook?

I'll use Google, Facebook, LinkedIn, Background/credit check, which means the person has to sign something. It may not be apparent, but sometimes, those are in small print on the bottom of an application that an employer asks you to fill out. I will do some of that before I decide to interviewer them. I usually don't do it afterwards, unless they said something during the interview that I wanted to explore. Somebody's politics should not be a reason why you hire or don't hire them. There was a woman who was not only politically opinionated, she was an activist. What does concern me is the amount of time someone is involved in political activity. If I had had an equal or stronger candidate, I would have gone with them. Interviewees need to be cautious about what information they share.

Are there any pet peeves you have that you've seen in an interview?

If somebody can't focus, that's a pet peeve. I interviewed somebody one time, and we had cork coasters in our conference room. While I was interviewing him, he was sitting with a pen putting dots on our cork coasters. I thought that was so unprofessional, that I stopped him.

Do you have any other advice?

Be 15 minutes early, it's better to wait until 5 minutes before your interview time before you actually go in because it can make the interviewer feel like they're scrambling if you're too early. On the other hand, there have been so many times people have called in saying "I can't find you" but you should have taken the time to find the location.

It's important that the candidate determine what the dress code is of the employer and at a minimum, meet that. It's better to be slightly above the minimum. If someone comes in and the office wears business casual, they should come in with a suit jacket on. If I wear Khakis and a polo, you wear khakis, polo, and a jacket.

Take it to the next level. Determine what the appropriate attire is for that workplace or office. If there's any question, it's better to be over dressed than under dressed.

Do not wear a cologne or perfume. At least go light on the perfume. You don't want to over power. Make sure you've showered, that your hair is washed, if you need a haircut. You don't want to do anything that is distracting.

Turn off your cell phone (leave it in the car). You don't want to distract the interviewer. If you have to keep it with you, turn it off.

Bring two copies of your resume at least. They should look professional, meaning on decent paper. I have seen resumes that look horrible because they were printed on crappy printers. If you have a bad printer, get them printed off at Kinkos. Good paper doesn't mean you have to get stationary stock, but don't put it on the cheap stuff you can practically see through, just a decent professional paper. That's a 5 to 6 dollar investment. If you're doing that and mailing resumes out, mail the cover letter with it.

If someone asks for a cover letter, make sure you write one. Don't just send a resume. They don't even get an interview, because if you can't follow the instructions, how can I expect you to do what I ask you to do in terms of job performance.

As an interviewer, there are two goals I have: goal one is to sell the company and opportunity, and I need to do that in a short period of time. As much as I'm looking for a candidate, the best candidate is also going to have other opportunities. I need to assess who is going to be the best person for this job. I had interviewed and hired people, and thought I was good at that. The second hire I made was not a good hire in the sense that before she started, I was going to be in DC [Washington DC]. I had asked her to come to one of our team meetings, so it would give us an opportunity to meet. She came, and the next day, she called and said she was sorry, but she can't do this.

The best way to determine future performance is to isolate past experiences that are relevant to the job I'm getting them to do. From a candidate's standpoint, the same thing holds true. So a candidate should ascertain the important elements of the job and explain how their life experiences are well suited for those things.

Establish a rapport with your interviewer. If you're interviewing in their office, take a look around. What are their interests? Do they have a family? Kids? It's tougher if you're interviewing in a conference room, but if you're in a conference room, the company usually has art, or a view. Use those things to build rapport.

With all of this, don't try to be somebody you're not because that is going to add additional strain and pressure that becomes evident to the interviewer. For example, if you're not the kind of person who tells jokes, don't go learn a joke just to break the ice. Stereotypes don't exist to the same degree as they did years ago. Interview while still being true to yourself.

Ask for a business card. Make sure you have the contact information for your interviewer, including the address. If you don't get that up front somehow before you're there, it becomes more difficult, and you won't be able to send a thank you card without that.

Finding out about a job is a fine balance of networking. Networking appropriately, which can be asking to meet somebody, to sit down and have coffee, or if they can provide some guidance for you as you're looking to start your career.

Along those lines, people need to be careful when they're just coming out of school. Happy hours can be a good place to network, but you don't want to drink too much.

Interview published with permission from Tarun Kundhi. Transcribed from phone interview, 5/19/2011.

Megan Metzer — President (Preferred Childcare)

How long have you been conducting professional interviews?

> 6 years

Roughly how many people have you interviewed during that time?

> 500 or so

Are there ways interviewees can ask engaging questions from their interviewer?

> Google interview questions, because a lot of companies use the same questions over and over again. Even if you print them out and think about them to focus your mind, it can go a long way. I don't have a problem if you need to take the time to think.

> The questions also depend on how the interview goes. Ask company-specific questions, like:

>> What qualities do you look for here?

>> What qualities are you looking for in your <job description>?

> Ask about the company's mission/vision if it's not transparent.

> I like a candidate that knows where they want to do. How do they see this job helping them get there? I don't like to hear someone without a plan. Having a plan means you're organized.

What are the major character traits you look for in an interviewee?

> Maturity is huge for us. We need someone that is mature, responsible, well-spoken, driven, and someone that wants to work with children for the rest of their lives. There are a lot of people looking for jobs. Make sure that you represent that this job is more than just a check to you. Honesty within reason; you don't have to share dark secrets. You need to be clear what you are comfortable with. I look for someone that is confident. Nervousness is one thing, but confidence will show through. I don't like to see waffling and equivocating, using vague language, that they aren't prepared for what I need them to do.

Are there any pet peeves you have that you've seen in an interview?

> Attire is really important. Showing up in a tank or tube top is not going to impress me at all. Take a shower and wash your hair before your interview. Wash your hair that morning, put on your deodorant. That is really important right off the bat.

> Waffling on answers

> If a candidate speaks negatively of their past employers, that's a huge red flag. If they're speaking negatively about this person, what will they say about us?

> Rambling on and over-talking. An interview is not the best time to do that.

> Chewing fingernails, Texting

Do you do any online background checks like Facebook, and Google?

> Yes, we do an actual background check. We Facebook them, and it's really important that they are on super-secret lockdown when it comes to sharing stuff on social media. If I'm trying to help a candidate, be on super-secret lock down. Use your privacy settings. I can tell a lot about somebody just looking at their picture. We also use Google.

Do you have any other advice?

> Someone can look fabulous on paper and sound great over the phone, but it's not until you meet them that you get a sense of what they are.

> Being late reflects extremely poorly, since most professionals are busy and stack interviews back to back. It's better to be on time or early even if the interviewer isn't ready. Tardiness cannot be tolerated in the industry. Do a dry run; make sure you can find the building. GPSs aren't 100% accurate and neither is map quest. Also, take a number with you, so you can call from the road.

> Dress nicely. Especially women must be aware not to show too much skin. No strong perfumes because it's distracting. Don't wear a ton of jewelry because it's flashy. Nothing low cut or skin tight.

> Use your cell phone with discretion. What' I've found with

college students is that they define an emergency different.

Always bring an extra copy of your resume to an interview. Make sure the resume is one page to make it as concise as possible. We don't need to know that you worked at burger king for two weeks when you were a junior in high school. Keep it as concise as possible and use a universal font like Arial or Times New Roman. Don't print it on pink paper or flowers trimming it. The cover letter should always list the company name.

Introduce yourself [to your interviewer]. Thank them for the opportunity. Smile. Listen intently. Eye contact is good, but don't stare them down. Small talk can help with nerves and the interviewer can automatically create a connection with the interviewee.

Have substance to your answers. Have a back story as to why you feel a certain way. Some interviewers may let you run the interview, so don't be so blunt that you leave them feeling some.

One question I feel every employer can ask: "If we were having this conversation 5 years from now, what would need to happen personally and professionally for you to be happy?" Be prepared to answer that.

I do see nervousness. Group interviews tend to automatically eliminate the nervousness. But on one-on-one, I sit them [interviewees] on a bench rather than across the desk. I know they get nervous, and I recognize that. I'll give them about 10 minutes to come out of their shell before I start judging the person.

Send thank you cards. It's huge. We've had people leave gifts. I think gifts are a little overboard. What I've always done is have Thank You notes in my car. Ask for a [business] card from the person you meet with. Fill out the Thank You note while you're in the parking lot and mail it out that day just in case they're making a quick decision. It takes two minutes, and it makes a world of difference.

Network! 85% of people I interview are from personal recommendations. Recommendations can get fast-tracked.

Interview published with permission from Megan Metzer. Transcribed from phone interview, 4/19/2011.

Josh Templeton — Regional Vice President (SaaS Company)

How long have you been conducting professional interviews?

>6 years

Roughly how many people have you interviewed during that time?

>50 people

Are there ways interviewees can ask engaging questions from their interviewer?

>Absolutely do some thoughtful research. The reason I say that is because you've got a competitive market place, and I'm looking for someone I can swap right into the position I'm looking for. If another candidate comes in with better questions, that tells me that that person took two minutes of their day to do some research and know what it is that we do.

>You need to have a minimum of 10 good questions because when you go through an interview, it's possible those questions will get answered during the course of the interview. It's better to be over-prepared and have more questions than you need.

>The research process is important because you get an understanding as to what the company is. It's a benefit for you as an interviewee because you'll know if you're a good fit. There is always a benefit to doing that first level research.

>Ask about the culture of the organization, and how they run their

business. What's the corporate philosophy? It will give the interviewee some insight about what makes the company tick.

How does the company do business? How does the company look at the market place? Are they focused on acquisitions? Do they focus on new clients? Do they grow it organically?

When they look at their biggest competitors, what are their strengths and weaknesses when it comes to them? How do they fit into the marketplace or against competitors?

Try to glean their mission statement. A 10Q document must be released by any publicly traded company along with their mission statement. There's a lot to be gleaned out of that document. [Find it on sec.gov]

Try to go off of recent press releases. Look for recent news and how that correlates to the position or how it correlates to the long term strategy.

The interview is as much for you as it is for them. It's definitely a balance.

Ask how they determine success outside of financial. Ask about KPIs (key performance indicators).

What are the major character traits you look for in an interviewee?

Positive, overcomers, articulate, composed, reflective

Are there any pet peeves you have that you've seen in an interview?

People that flirt is a major pet peeve.

I hate when someone has done zero research. They come into the interview and waste my time. I've cut interviews short when it's evident that a person has not done appropriate research.

Inappropriate behavior is never appreciated.

No thank you note or no thank you email.

Is there any other advice you'd give a potential candidate?

In today's market place, you need to be honest in your skill sets. If you're creative in the interview process, when you get into negotiations of salary, there are sign on bonuses, vacation time.

Golden rule in face to face interview, When's someone's walking in. The first thing I'm looking for is clean cut, somebody I can take and put in front of my grandmother and CEO of fortune 500 company. Simple, simple, simple, keep it visually simple. Make sure your shoes are polished. With regards to aesthetics, I look for people that have nicer watches, attaché because it indicates previous business experience or they recognize that they must look the part. A watch is not necessarily a bad thing. Typically the interview is very engaging, and you won't have a problem checking your watch. Don't glance at your watch. Semantics.

Always bring an extra copy of your resume to an interview. Sometimes companies will interview you, go through the process, like you, and walk you into another room. Bring a couple copies of your resume because it is always easier to have two than it is to have one. Make it look like an important document and treat it like an important document. Keep it in a manila folder with your name on it.

It's such a delicate art to create business rapport and one of the most difficult things to do. Some people do it naturally, some need to learn it.

Go in, always be yourself and try to find that commonality. Be open about yourself without revealing everything. Maybe before you get started, offer a personal experience. Whenever you look at interviewees that do well, they look at interviewees, tenure, and success they've had. They use those people as evaluation criteria. The people that do well, they build rapport, and they explain things well. They pause, and tie in a story and experience into that particular question. The conversation becomes much more compelling when you have stories to back up your answers.

You want the interviewer to understand who you are and that you're multi-faceted. The ones that do well open up and talk about themselves. It becomes much more difficult for the interviewer to be difficult because there's a human component there.

Send thank you cards. It is as rare like the dodo bird.

Interview 101: People are afraid to ask the questions. For

example: do you think based off our conversation today, that potentially I'd be a good fit for your organization? They [interviewees] don't ask the basic questions and walk away wondering. Don't be afraid to ask them. It's a trial close. Come out and ask if the interview went well. People will shoot you straight. If they stammer or don't say anything, follow up with "Do you have any concerns about me taking a position on your organization?" That will allow you to address any concerns then. Questions are your friend. You always want to ask open ended questions that are probing. When you ask a question, make sure the answer isn't yes, no, or number. It defeats the point of asking a question. The point is to gain insight and create dialog.

When someone goes into an interview, they need to treat it as if they're at the doctor's. A patient comes in, they've got a problem. The patient is concerned they have a problem, so the doctor must ask good questions to get to the bottom of it. They ask questions that lead them down the trail. They gain insight, so at the end of it, they can assimilate the information.

People should treat the interview with the perspective of a doctor and dig deeper as opposed to just scratching the surface. More senior associates tend to do that well. Interviewing isn't some dark art. It's just presenting yourself well and allowing your special characteristics and attributes shine.

Interview published with permission from Josh Templeton. Transcribed from phone interview, 4/28/2011.

Negotiation Expert

Bill Davis — Negotiations Expert (University Professor)

How many job candidates seem to understand and take advantage of their professional value during the salary negotiation?

> If you're asking how many now negotiate, that number (percentage) is increasing with all the attention to the need to negotiate salary. However, if you are asking about value, I'm not sure that many folks do a good job of determining their personal/professional value, nor do they understand the limitations that position value places on what they might be compensated for a particular role in a specific company, industry, location, etc. One wants to determine her personal value—what one brings to the job—from experience, credentials, etc. However, no organization will pay above what a position is worth to them; if they did, they would lose money.

What are key considerations candidates often don't consider when negotiating their salary?

> They typically have one job offer in hand. They need to have two or more (including staying where they are) if they really want to have any bargaining power. So, if they only have one job offer, they need to go get more, if possible, before negotiating. Secondly, candidates often compare the offer they are getting to their current compensation. Two problems: one is that the job they currently have may have little comparison to the

job they are seeking. They need to value themselves and the future role for what they are; not a comfortable percentage increase over what they are currently making. Two is that candidates often compare the salary of the new job with what they are currently making right now... not six months from now when they would be receiving a 3–4% increase if they stayed with their current employer.

What are some of the common ways candidates can increase their BATNA before a salary negotiation takes place?

Well, I've already mentioned one: get other offers; don't just look at one potential employer at a time. They need to know what they are worth in the marketplace and, I think, the best way to do that is to look at the annual salary survey data of their professional associations. Don't have any professional memberships? Get them. These are better—more accurate, more persuasive, more objective—than Internet sites. If headhunters are calling you, follow the process long enough to see what the market is doing.

What not to do!! Don't go looking for a job, get an offer, negotiate the offer, and then go to your current firm and tell them that you have another offer—expecting that they will give you a counteroffer, which will serve as your BATNA. If you were to do that to me as your manager, I would wish you well and send you on your way.

Would being nervous in a salary negotiation hurt someone's chance of getting a better deal, or does nervousness not have much of an impact?

Some nervousness is expected; in fact, someone who is too confident in a selection interview might come across as arrogant. I would be more concerned about answering the questions being asked, about asking good, relevant questions of the interviewer which show that you have done your homework and that you are truly knowledgeable about the field, the company, the role, etc. Now, talking about your nerves is a no, no; that not only makes you appear nervous, but also weak and self-conscious.

What's the biggest risk of asking for too much money at the start?

For one thing, it's the wrong timing, and it's not your turn. We don't negotiate compensation until we have been extended an offer by the hiring manager. That shouldn't happen until both parties are very sure that they want to "get married." If salary comes up too early, you—as the candidate—should indicate that it is premature and that you would rather wait until the parties have determined they want to proceed to that step. I know this is becoming more and more difficult—especially when working through headhunters who want to "qualify" a candidate before recommending him/her for consideration. However, salary is irrelevant if the job is not a fit for one or both parties. Neither party will know that unless they invest some time in getting to know each other.

Interview published with permission from Bill Davis. Sent via email, 6/16/2015

About the Author

Austin F. Fadely grew up a native of Southern Maryland and attended undergrad in Baltimore at UMBC, where he majored in English Communications with minors in History and Psychology. After spending several years as a textbook writer and editor, Austin moved to Winston-Salem, NC. Around that time, he shifted careers and became a project manager for software design and development.

Austin attended Wake Forest University, where he earned his MBA. In late 2014, Austin returned to the DC area to take up consulting.

In 2015, Austin started on a mission to teach students and young professionals lifelong success skills that will guide them through college and the work force. Austin currently lives in Northern Virginia with his wife and three children.